HOW TO FLIRT IN
UKRAINIAN

YOUR GUIDE TO DATING AND FLIRTING IN UKRAINIAN

BY

ADRIAN GEE

ISBN: 979-8-300241-25-4

Copyright © 2024 by Adrian Gee.

All rights reserved.

No part of this book may be reproduced, stored in a retrieval system, or transmitted in any form or by any means, electronic, mechanical, photocopying, recording, scanning, or otherwise, without the prior written permission of the publisher.

AUTHOR'S NOTE

Welcome to *How to Flirt in Ukrainian!* I'm beyond excited to share this book with you and be your companion on the journey of learning how to flirt, connect, and communicate in Ukrainian. Whether you're looking to charm someone special or navigate social situations with confidence, this book is here to make your learning fun, interactive, and effective.

This book is what happens when a passion for languages meets an interest in dating and connection. Combining the best of both worlds, I've crafted this resource to help you bridge language gaps and create moments that are memorable and meaningful.

Connect with Me: Language learning is more than memorizing words—it's about building bridges between people and cultures. I'd love for you to join me on this journey. Follow me on Instagram: @adriangruszka, and check out my website at www.adriangee.com for more tips, stories, and language-learning resources. Share your progress, ask questions, and be part of a supportive community that loves learning and connecting.

Sharing is Caring: If you find *How to Flirt in Ukrainian* helpful, consider sharing it with your friends or fellow language enthusiasts. I'd be delighted to see your achievements and moments using what you've learned! Tag me on Instagram, and I'll happily share your posts with my audience.

Learning a language is a rewarding adventure that opens up new possibilities and connections. Embrace the journey, celebrate the small wins, and most importantly, have fun exploring the language of love and laughter.

Удачі та насолоджуйтесь! (Good luck and enjoy!)

- *Adrian Gee*

CONTENTS

Introduction 1
Chapter One: The Language of Flirting 7
The Foundations of Flirting Vocabulary 8
Building Confidence with Greetings and Introductions 12
The Art of Giving and Receiving Compliments 18
Putting It All Together: The First Flirt 25
Chapter Two: Pickup Lines 33
The Art of the Pickup Line 34
Categories of Pickup Lines 40
Adapting Pickup Lines to Different Environments 46
The Dos and Don'ts of Using Pickup Lines 53
Personalized Pickup Lines Based on Shared Interests 60
Chapter Three: Formal vs. Informal Flirting 69
The Role of Tone: Formal vs. Informal Flirting 70
Vocabulary for Formal vs. Informal Flirting 76
Flirting in Professional vs. Social Environments 80
Formal and Informal Flirting Dialogues in Action 87
Practice Exercises: Testing Formal vs. Informal Flirting Skills ... 93
Chapter Four: Dating Vocabulary and Useful Phrases 101
Essential Vocabulary for Dating and Relationships 102
Complimenting Your Date: Phrases to Make an Impression ... 106
Expressing Interest and Making Plans 110
Conversation Starters and Keeping the Conversation Going ... 115
Phrases for Showing Affection and Building a Connection 120
Dealing with Misunderstandings and Awkward Moments 124
Navigating Boundaries and Relationship Expectations 129
Phrases for Ending Dates or Conversations Gracefully 134
Digital Flirting: Building Connections Through Text 138
Ending Relationships Politely 144
Chapter Five: Conversations & Dialogues 149
Meeting Someone for the First Time 150
Small Talk: Keeping it Light and Fun 154
Making Plans Together 159

Deepening the Conversation: Moving Beyond Small Talk 164
Flirting Through Text and Social Media 168
Handling Awkward Moments and Misunderstandings 172
Talking About Hobbies and Interests 176
Navigating Emotional Conversations 180
Chapter Six: Compliments and Responses 185
Making a Great First Impression 186
Compliments on Personality: Going Beyond Looks 190
How to Accept Compliments Gracefully 193
Compliments for Specific Interests and Achievements 196
Flirting with Questions: Keeping the Conversation Going 200
Chapter Seven: Handling Rejection 207
Understanding Rejection: The Reality of Dating 208
Responding with Grace and Positivity 211
Maintaining Self-Confidence Post-Rejection 215
Setting Boundaries and Respecting Others' Decisions 219
Turning Rejection into a Positive Experience 222
Moving Forward: Embracing New Opportunities 225
Chapter Eight: Fun Quizzes and Flirting Challenges 229
What's Your Flirting Style? 230
Build Your Own Flirty Conversation 235
First Date Icebreaker Game 240
Chapter Nine: Putting It All Together 245

INTRODUCTION

Welcome to *How to Flirt in Ukrainian*, a fun, light-hearted guide to help you navigate the often mysterious world of dating and flirting in one of the world's most beautiful and underrated languages—Ukrainian! Whether you're just starting out or have some experience with the language, this book is designed to make flirting in Ukrainian feel effortless, enjoyable, and most importantly, natural. This isn't just a vocabulary book, nor is it merely a list of generic phrases. Instead, it's an immersive journey that will boost your confidence in striking up conversations, paying compliments, and navigating romantic encounters, all in Ukrainian.

When we think of flirting, it's easy to picture clever one-liners and witty comebacks, but flirting is about so much more. It's an art form, a dance of words and body language that often reveals more about our personality and intent than we realize. And when you're flirting in a second language like Ukrainian, the stakes feel a bit higher, but don't worry—we've got you covered.

PURPOSE OF THE BOOK

The goal of *How to Flirt in Ukrainian* is simple: to help you flirt and communicate confidently in Ukrainian-speaking environments. Whether you're traveling to Ukraine, looking to connect with a Ukrainian-speaking romantic interest, or just want to have fun learning a new language skill, this book will provide you with the tools to succeed. You don't have to be fluent in Ukrainian to be charming! Even knowing a few phrases and conversational techniques can help you break the ice and leave a lasting impression.

Through a mix of carefully chosen pickup lines, authentic dialogues, cultural insights, and practical exercises, this book will walk you through different social scenarios, from meeting someone at a bar to striking up a conversation in a café, and even flirting on dating apps. We've made sure to include both formal and informal approaches, because flirting in Ukrainian is as much about knowing when to use the right tone as it is about knowing the right words. By the end of this book, you'll feel at ease whether you're dropping a casual compliment or expressing sincere interest in someone special.

WHAT TO EXPECT

One of the unique aspects of flirting in Ukrainian is the deep connection it has with cultural values and traditions. A charming phrase that wins hearts in Kyiv might not resonate the same way in Lviv or Odessa. That's why this book delves into the cultural richness of Ukrainian flirting—helping you grasp the nuances of various regions. From the Carpathian Mountains to the Black Sea coast, we'll uncover how local traditions influence romantic interactions, enabling you to adapt your approach to fit each context. Understanding these cultural subtleties will not only make your flirting more natural but will also create a more meaningful connection with the person you're interested in.

But this book isn't just about theory—it's packed with practical examples and exercises to help you practice and perfect your flirting skills. Each chapter includes useful pickup lines, complete dialogues for different environments (like bars, cafés, and online), and a step-by-step guide to navigating romantic situations in Ukrainian. You'll find exercises that will encourage you to try out these lines, either with a language partner or even in real-life settings. The more you practice, the more natural it will feel.

CONFIDENCE AT ANY LEVEL

Flirting can be intimidating, especially in a second language, but rest assured, this book is designed for all levels. If you're a beginner, don't worry—we'll start with the basics, introducing simple phrases and vocabulary that anyone can master. You'll gradually build your skills through a series of fun and interactive exercises, so by the time you reach the more advanced sections, you'll feel confident in your ability to charm in Ukrainian.

For those with a bit more experience in the language, this book offers more nuanced strategies and tips on how to elevate your flirting game. We'll cover everything from witty comebacks to subtle compliments and even how to handle rejection gracefully, all while helping you expand your Ukrainian vocabulary in the process.

FLIRTING WITH PURPOSE

Flirting, in any language, is about connection. It's about showing interest in someone, making them smile, and sparking that initial conversation that could lead to something more. By using the tools in this book, you'll not only learn how to flirt in Ukrainian, but you'll also gain a deeper understanding of how language and culture influence romantic interactions. You'll find that the more comfortable you become with the language, the more confident you'll feel, not just in flirting, but in communicating in general.

Whether you're planning a romantic getaway to Ukraine or just want to impress someone on a date, *How to Flirt in Ukrainian* will give you the confidence and skills to make your mark. So, get ready to explore a world where words are just as important as actions, where culture meets romance, and where learning Ukrainian becomes more than just a language lesson—it becomes an adventure in connection, charm, and fun.

So, are you ready to master the art of flirting in Ukrainian? Let's dive in and discover just how easy—and enjoyable—it can be!

CHAPTER ONE:
THE LANGUAGE OF FLIRTING

THE FOUNDATIONS OF FLIRTING VOCABULARY

When learning to flirt in Ukrainian, a strong foundation in key vocabulary related to flirting, attraction, and dating is essential. Knowing how to express your interest clearly and confidently can open the door to deeper conversations and connections. In this section, we'll introduce you to some essential words and phrases that you'll use repeatedly in romantic scenarios. Whether you're giving a compliment, asking someone out, or simply showing your admiration, these words will help you flirt with ease.

Key Vocabulary: The Building Blocks of Flirting

Let's start with the core words you'll need in any romantic or dating situation. These words will form the foundation for everything from casual compliments to more serious expressions of interest.

- **Фліртувати (verb): To flirt.**
  Example: Мені подобається фліртувати з тобою.
  (I like flirting with you.)

- **Гарний/красива (adjective): Handsome/beautiful.**
  Example: Ти дуже гарний/красива.
  (You're very handsome/beautiful.)

- **Привабливість (noun): Attraction.**
  Example: Я відчуваю сильну привабливість до тебе.
  (I feel a strong attraction to you.)

- **Побачення (noun)**: Date.
  Example: У нас сьогодні ввечері побачення.
  (We have a date tonight.)

- **Чарівний/чарівна (adjective)**: Charming.
  Example: Ти дуже чарівний/чарівна.
  (You're very charming.)

- **Романтичний/романтична (adjective)**: Romantic.
  Example: Мені подобається твоя романтична сторона.
  (I like your romantic side.)

These words are great for laying the groundwork in any flirtatious conversation. They're not only useful for speaking directly to someone you're interested in but also when describing your feelings to others.

Essential Phrases to Show Interest

Now that you have some of the key vocabulary down, it's time to learn how to put these words into action with a few simple but effective phrases. These can be used to show interest, pay a compliment, or express admiration. Remember, don't forget to add a smile and a confident tone!

- **Я люблю твою усмішку.**
  (I love your smile.)

    A great opener when you want to compliment someone on their appearance in a non-intimidating way. This simple phrase can break the ice.

- **Хочеш якось піти кудись разом?**
  (Would you like to go out sometime?)

  This is a direct but polite way to ask someone on a date. It's clear and respectful, making it a go-to phrase for initiating plans with someone you're interested in.

- **У тебе красиві очі.**
  (You have beautiful eyes.)

  Complimenting someone's eyes is a classic and often successful approach. It's specific enough to feel personal but still light-hearted enough to be appropriate in most settings.

- **Ти неймовірно гарний/красива.**
  (You're incredibly handsome/beautiful.)

  If you want to be direct with your admiration, this phrase is bold yet complimentary. It works well in more informal or relaxed environments.

- **Я хотів/хотіла б краще тебе пізнати.**
  (I'd love to get to know you better.)

  This is perfect when you want to express interest in continuing the conversation beyond your first meeting. It's respectful but also leaves room for the other person to decide how they'd like to proceed.

Using the Vocabulary in Different Settings

Context matters a lot when flirting in Ukrainian, and it's important to adjust your approach based on where and how the conversation is taking place. For example, if you're in a casual setting like a café or bar, you might lean more on informal and playful phrases. In contrast, if you're at a formal event, you might want to keep things polite and less forward.

- In a **café** or **restaurant**, starting with a compliment like *Я люблю твою усмішку* is perfect for easing into the conversation.

- At a **bar** or **nightclub**, you can be a bit more playful with a phrase like *Ти неймовірно гарний/красива* if the atmosphere is light and informal.

- In **online dating** or over text, phrases like *Я хотів/хотіла б краще тебе пізнати* are useful to show sincere interest while maintaining some casual distance.

BUILDING CONFIDENCE WITH GREETINGS AND INTRODUCTIONS

Flirting often begins with the simplest form of communication: a greeting. How you start a conversation sets the tone for the interaction, and first impressions are key, especially when you're trying to connect with someone romantically. Whether you're introducing yourself in a formal or informal setting, knowing the right greeting and maintaining confidence can make all the difference. In this section, we'll explore how to greet someone confidently in Ukrainian, ask the right questions, and use body language to enhance your words.

The Importance of First Impressions

First impressions are lasting, and when it comes to flirting, they can either open the door to a meaningful connection or shut it down before things even get started. A confident, friendly greeting shows interest and warmth, making the other person feel comfortable and intrigued.

In Ukrainian culture, greetings often reflect the social context. Is the setting formal or informal? Are you meeting the person for the first time, or is it a more casual situation? Knowing how to adapt your greeting based on these factors will help you navigate different environments with ease.

Formal vs. Informal Greetings

In Ukrainian, there are distinctions between formal and informal greetings, depending on the situation and the level of familiarity you have with the person. Let's break down the differences:

1. **Informal Greeting: Привіт**

    - *Привіт* (hello) is the go-to informal greeting in Ukrainian. It's friendly, approachable, and perfect for casual settings. Whether you're at a party, bar, or café, *Привіт* works well as an icebreaker.

    - Example:

        - **Привіт, як справи?**
          (Hi, how are you?)

        - **Привіт, мене звати [Ваше ім'я].**
          (Hi, my name is [Your Name].)

2. **Formal Greeting: Доброго ранку, доброго дня, доброго вечора**

    - For more formal situations—such as meeting someone for the first time at an event or speaking to someone older—use time-specific greetings like *Доброго ранку* (good morning), *Доброго дня* (good afternoon), or *Доброго вечора* (good evening).

- Example:

  - **Доброго ранку, як вас звати?**
    (Good morning, what's your name?)

  - **Доброго дня, приємно познайомитися.**
    (Good afternoon, it's a pleasure to meet you.)

Using the right greeting shows that you respect the social setting and the other person's position, which can go a long way in leaving a positive impression.

Common Questions for First Encounters

After your greeting, it's essential to follow up with questions that keep the conversation flowing. These questions should be simple but open-ended enough to invite more dialogue. Let's look at a few key questions that will help you continue the conversation:

- **Як тебе звати?**
  (What's your name?)

  A basic but essential question that starts most first encounters. It's also a great way to break the ice if you're nervous about initiating the conversation.

- **Звідки ти?**
  (Where are you from?)

  This question not only sparks conversation but also gives you an opportunity to learn more about the person's background. It's a friendly way to show interest without being too forward.

- **Що привело тебе сюди?**
  (What brings you here?)

  This question is particularly useful in social settings like parties or events. It helps transition the conversation into talking about common interests or mutual friends.

- **Чим ти займаєшся (працюєш/навчаєшся)?**
  (What do you do for work/study?)

  Asking about their job or studies is a polite way to learn more about their life. Just make sure to keep the tone light and don't turn it into a formal interview.

These basic questions can help you steer the conversation while allowing the other person to open up about themselves. They also give you clues about how to direct the conversation further.

The Role of Body Language

While words are important, how you carry yourself during an introduction can make a significant difference in how you're perceived. Non-verbal communication—such as body language, eye contact, and even subtle gestures—can enhance your flirting efforts and make your words more meaningful.

- **Maintaining Eye Contact**

    Eye contact is a powerful tool in flirting. It shows confidence and interest. When introducing yourself, maintain eye contact to convey sincerity and attraction. Just be sure not to overdo it; alternating between eye contact and looking away shows naturalness and prevents the interaction from feeling too intense.

- **Smiling**

    A genuine smile can be one of the most inviting gestures. Smiling as you introduce yourself helps set a friendly and warm tone. It shows that you're approachable and engaged.

- **Light Touches (When Appropriate)**

    In Ukrainian culture, light touches (like a brief touch on the arm or shoulder) can be a natural part of conversation. It's important to gauge the situation, though—start with subtle touches if the environment feels comfortable and the other person seems receptive. If you sense hesitation, it's best to refrain.

- **Open Posture**

    Keep your body language open. Facing the person directly with relaxed shoulders signals that you're interested and fully engaged. Avoid crossing your arms, as this can appear closed off or disinterested.

By using body language to complement your words, you add depth to the conversation, making your introduction feel more authentic and engaging.

THE ART OF GIVING AND RECEIVING COMPLIMENTS

Giving a compliment is one of the easiest and most effective ways to flirt, but knowing how and when to deliver that compliment can make all the difference. In Ukrainian culture, compliments are often seen as a natural part of social interaction, especially in flirting and dating. Whether it's complimenting someone's appearance or admiring their personality, the key is to be genuine and respectful. In this section, we'll explore how to give romantic and sincere compliments in Ukrainian, the best moments to use them, and how to respond graciously when receiving a compliment.

Romantic Compliments: Admiring Someone's Appearance

When it comes to romantic compliments, Ukrainian offers a range of expressions that can make someone feel special and appreciated. Whether you're commenting on someone's physical beauty or admiring their style, the goal is to be respectful and sincere. Let's start with a few classic compliments that focus on someone's appearance.

- **У тебе красиві очі.**
  (You have beautiful eyes.)

  This is a timeless compliment that focuses on a specific and attractive feature. Complimenting someone's eyes is a subtle yet effective way to show admiration, without being overly forward. It works well in both casual and more intimate conversations.

- **Ти неймовірно гарний/красива.**
  (You're incredibly handsome/beautiful.)

This is a more direct and bold compliment, ideal for when you feel comfortable being open about your attraction. The word "*гарний*" is typically used for men, while "*красива*" is more common for women. Depending on the setting, you can use this phrase to express sincere admiration in a flattering way.

- **Мені подобається твій стиль.**
  (I love your style.)

Complimenting someone's sense of style is another great way to break the ice. It shows that you've noticed something unique about them, which can make the compliment feel more personal.

- **У тебе чарівна усмішка.**
  (You have a charming smile.)

Complimenting someone's smile is universally appreciated, and it can create an instant connection. This phrase is perfect for keeping the conversation light and playful.

These romantic compliments are effective because they highlight features in a flattering yet respectful manner. It's important to remember that timing and delivery are just as crucial as the words themselves.

Sincere Compliments: Admiring Someone's Personality

While romantic compliments focus on physical appearance, sincere compliments about someone's personality can create a deeper connection. By acknowledging their inner qualities, you show that you're interested in more than just looks, which can make your compliments more meaningful.

- **Мені подобається розмовляти з тобою.**
  (I love talking to you.)

  This phrase is simple yet powerful. It tells the person that you enjoy their company and value the conversation, making them feel appreciated on a deeper level. This compliment is great for when you've been talking for a while and want to express your interest without being too forward.

- **У тебе чудове почуття гумору.**
  (You have a fantastic sense of humor.)

  Laughter is often a key component in flirting, and complimenting someone's sense of humor is a great way to show that you're enjoying their presence. This compliment works well in both casual and romantic contexts.

- **Ти дуже цікава людина.**
  (You're a very interesting person.)

  Complimenting someone's intellect or unique qualities can make them feel valued beyond surface-level attraction. It opens the door to deeper conversations and shows that you're genuinely interested in getting to know them.

- **Ти викликаєш у мене багато довіри.**
  (You inspire a lot of trust in me.)

  This compliment is more serious and works well in situations where you want to show that you value trust and honesty in your connection. It can be particularly effective when the conversation has moved beyond casual flirting and into a more meaningful exchange.

By mixing these romantic and sincere compliments, you can create a balanced approach to flirting that shows genuine interest in both appearance and personality.

Timing and Cultural Context: When and How to Use Compliments

The key to giving compliments lies not only in what you say but also in when and how you say it. In Ukrainian culture, compliments are common, but their impact can vary depending on the context. Here are a few tips on how to use compliments effectively:

1. **Start Light**

    When meeting someone for the first time, start with lighter compliments, such as commenting on their smile or style. Compliments that are too personal or intimate early on can feel overwhelming, especially if the other person isn't ready for that level of attention. For example, *Я люблю твою усмішку* (I love your smile) is a perfect way to ease into the conversation.

2. **Consider the Setting**

    Flirting at a casual party might call for playful compliments, whereas a more formal event may require subtlety and politeness. In more formal settings, a compliment like *У тебе чарівна усмішка* (You have a charming smile) is polite but still flirtatious. In informal environments, you can be more direct with phrases like *Ти неймовірно гарний/красива* (You're incredibly handsome/beautiful).

3. Be Mindful of Cultural Differences

   In Ukraine, the way compliments are given and received can vary depending on the region and the cultural setting. In larger cities like Kyiv or Odessa, people may be more open and playful with compliments, while in smaller towns or more traditional areas, compliments might be considered more personal and intimate. Understanding these differences can help you approach romantic interactions with sensitivity and respect.

4. Use Body Language to Reinforce Your Words

   Compliments are often more effective when paired with positive body language. Maintaining eye contact and offering a genuine smile can enhance the impact of your words, making the compliment feel more authentic.

Responding to Compliments: Accepting with Grace

Just as important as giving compliments is learning how to respond to them. In Ukrainian culture, compliments are often met with gratitude, but it's important to respond in a way that feels natural to you. Here are a few common ways to acknowledge and respond to compliments:

- **Дякую, ти дуже добрий/добра.**
  (Thank you, you're very kind.)

  This is a polite and classic response to most compliments. It shows that you appreciate the gesture without drawing too much attention to the

- **Ти змушуєш мене червоніти.**
  (You're making me blush.)

  If you want to respond in a playful way, this phrase adds a light-hearted touch while acknowledging the compliment.

- **Це так мило з твого боку.**
  (That's so sweet of you.)

  Another warm and friendly response, perfect for compliments that are particularly thoughtful.

Remember that responding to a compliment is about accepting it graciously, without downplaying or deflecting the positive attention. Confidence is key in both giving and receiving compliments!

PUTTING IT ALL TOGETHER: THE FIRST FLIRT

Now that you've learned the vocabulary, phrases, and non-verbal cues that make flirting in Ukrainian effective, it's time to put it all into practice. In this section, we'll combine what you've learned into a realistic flirting scenario and break down each part of the conversation to show why it works. Whether you're meeting someone in a café or having a playful chat at a party, knowing how to engage with confidence is key to successful flirting.

We'll start with a full dialogue example of a casual encounter at a café and then break down why each phrase and non-verbal cue works in context. Finally, we'll end with an exercise where you can practice your own dialogue, either by yourself or with a partner.

Scenario: Meeting Someone at a Café

Imagine you've just walked into a café, and after ordering your coffee, you notice someone sitting nearby who catches your eye. You want to start a conversation in a relaxed and natural way, without being too forward. Here's how you could approach the situation.

Dialogue Example:

You: Привіт, можна сісти тут?
(Hi, can I sit here?)

Them: Звичайно, сідай.
(Sure, go ahead.)

You: Дякую. Мене звати [Ваше ім'я], а як тебе звати?
(Thank you. My name is [Your Name], what's your name?)

Them: Мене звати [Їхнє ім'я].
(My name is [Their Name].)

You: Приємно познайомитися, [Їхнє ім'я]. Ти часто приходиш у це кафе?
(Nice to meet you, [Their Name]. Do you come to this café often?)

Them: Так, мені дуже подобається це місце. Тут спокійно, і кава дуже смачна.
(Yes, I really like this place. It's quiet, and the coffee is really good.)

You: Згоден/згодна, тут найкраща кава в районі. До того ж, мені подобається атмосфера. Це гарне місце, щоб відпочити й познайомитися з цікавими людьми.
(I agree, they have the best coffee in the area. Plus, I love the atmosphere here. It's a good place to relax and meet interesting people.)

Them: Так, точно. Тут завжди є цікаві люди.
(Yes, definitely. There are always interesting people here.)

You: До речі, у тебе чарівна усмішка.
(By the way, you have a lovely smile.)

Them: Дякую, це так люб'язно з твого боку.
(Thank you, how kind of you.)

You: Будь ласка. Що ти любиш робити у вільний час?
(You're welcome. What do you like to do in your free time?)

Them: Ну, я люблю читати, а ще мені подобається гуляти містом. А ти?
(Well, I love reading and I also enjoy walking around the city. What about you?)

You: Мені теж подобається гуляти, особливо в парку. Це чудовий спосіб розслабитися. Можливо, якось прогуляємось разом?
(I also enjoy walking, especially through the park. It's a great way to unwind. Maybe we could take a walk together sometime.)

Them: Я б із задоволенням.
(I'd love that.)

Breaking Down the Conversation

Let's take a closer look at why each part of this conversation works and how it uses the flirting techniques you've learned so far.

1. Starting with a Simple Question

    - **Привіт, можна сісти тут?**
      (Hi, can I sit here?)

      Starting with a polite question helps ease into the conversation without being too forward. It's non-threatening and creates an opportunity to continue the dialogue naturally.

2. Introducing Yourself with Confidence

    - **Мене звати [Ваше ім'я], а як тебе звати?**
      (My name is [Your Name], what's your name?)

      Introducing yourself early in the conversation shows confidence and interest. Asking for their name immediately creates a more personal connection.

3. Light, Casual Small Talk

    - **Ти часто приходиш у це кафе?**
      (Do you come to this café often?)

      This is a great, non-intimidating way to keep the conversation going. It's a casual question that leads naturally into discussing shared interests.

4. Sharing a Common Interest

- **Згоден/згодна, тут найкраща кава в районі. До того ж, мені подобається атмосфера. Це гарне місце, щоб відпочити й познайомитися з цікавими людьми.**
  (I agree, they have the best coffee in the area. Plus, I love the atmosphere here. It's a good place to relax and meet interesting people.)

  Sharing your own thoughts about the café creates a sense of commonality. It also subtly indicates that you're open to meeting new people, setting the tone for further conversation.

5. Giving a Compliment

- **До речі, у тебе чарівна усмішка.**
  (By the way, you have a lovely smile.)

  This is a simple, flattering compliment that adds a bit of flirtation without being too forward. It's light and respectful, which makes it appropriate for a first encounter.

6. Asking About Their Interests

- **Що ти любиш робити у вільний час?**
  (What do you like to do in your free time?)

  Asking about their hobbies or interests is a great way to show genuine curiosity. It keeps the conversation flowing and opens the door to finding more common ground.

7. **Suggesting a Future Plan**

    - **Можливо, якось прогуляємось разом?**
      (Maybe we could take a walk together sometime.)

      This is a subtle way to suggest spending more time together. It's not too pushy and offers an easy, casual option for a future encounter.

Exercise: Practice the Dialogue

Now that you've seen how to combine everything into a smooth conversation, it's time to practice. In this exercise, you'll create your own version of the dialogue or practice it with a partner. The goal is to use the vocabulary, phrases, and flirting techniques you've learned to create a natural, engaging conversation.

1. **Create Your Own Dialogue**

    Choose a setting (café, party, park, etc.) and write out a conversation where you meet someone new. Make sure to include:

    - A polite question to start the conversation.
    - An introduction with your name.
    - Light small talk to keep the conversation flowing.
    - A compliment.
    - A question about their interests or hobbies.
    - A casual suggestion for spending time together in the future.

2. Practice with a Partner

   If possible, practice the dialogue with a friend or language partner. One person will play the role of starting the conversation, while the other responds. Focus on using the correct vocabulary, keeping the conversation natural, and incorporating non-verbal cues like eye contact and smiling.

3. Adjust and Reflect

   After practicing, think about what worked well and what felt awkward. Did the conversation flow naturally? Did you feel confident giving a compliment? Adjust your approach as needed and practice again.

Mastering the art of flirting in Ukrainian takes practice, but by combining the vocabulary and techniques you've learned, you can approach conversations with confidence. Remember, flirting is as much about listening and responding as it is about what you say. The more you practice, the more natural it will feel.

CHAPTER TWO:
PICKUP LINES

THE ART OF THE PICKUP LINE

Pickup lines have long been a staple of flirtation, offering a light-hearted and often humorous way to break the ice. When used effectively, a well-placed pickup line can instantly grab someone's attention, make them smile, or even spark a deeper conversation. However, the art of the pickup line lies in its delicate balance between playfulness and respect. It's a fine line between charming and cringeworthy, and understanding that balance is key to successful flirting.

In this section, we'll explore what makes a good pickup line, how cultural context plays a role in their effectiveness, and break down examples of famous pickup lines in both English and Ukrainian. We'll also dive into the key elements that make a pickup line work: humor, compliments, confidence, and cultural awareness.

What Makes a Good Pickup Line?

At its core, a good pickup line is all about creating a connection. Whether through humor, a sincere compliment, or a clever turn of phrase, the goal is to initiate a conversation in a way that feels natural, not forced. A great pickup line is light-hearted, playful, and most importantly, respectful of the other person's comfort level. The best lines make the person smile or laugh, but never at their expense.

What separates a successful pickup line from a cheesy or awkward one is how it's delivered. The tone, confidence, and timing all matter just as much as the words themselves. A good pickup line is rarely just about what you say—it's about how you say it.

Cultural Context: Flirting Across Borders

When flirting in a Ukrainian context, it's important to be aware of the cultural nuances that can shape how your words are perceived. In some settings, flirtation in Ukraine may be more reserved and sincere, while in others, especially among younger generations or in urban areas, it can be playful and lighthearted. For instance, in cities like Kyiv or Lviv, people might respond well to witty and humorous compliments, while in more traditional or rural areas, a genuine and respectful approach is often preferred.

For example, a playful pickup line like "*Чи ти чарівниця? Бо коли ти поруч, світ стає яскравішим.*" (Are you a magician? Because when you're around, the world feels brighter.) might work well in a casual and relaxed setting in a modern café or social event. On the other hand, in a more formal or traditional setting, a sincere compliment such as "*У тебе дуже гарна усмішка.*" (You have a very beautiful smile.) would likely be more appropriate and appreciated.

By understanding the social context and cultural expectations, you can navigate romantic interactions with ease and ensure that your flirting leaves a positive impression.

Famous Pickup Lines: English vs. Ukrainian

To get a better sense of how pickup lines work, let's look at a few famous or commonly used lines in both English and Ukrainian. By comparing these, we can break down what makes them effective, funny, or charming.

English Example:

- **Did it hurt? When you fell from heaven?**

    This classic line works because it's playful and humorous, relying on a metaphor to give a compliment. It's slightly cheesy, but it's delivered in a light-hearted way that makes it clear the speaker isn't taking themselves too seriously.

Ukrainian Example:

- **Ти віриш у кохання з першого погляду, чи мені пройти повз ще раз?**
    (Do you believe in love at first sight, or should I walk by again?)

    This line, much like its English counterpart, is playful and a bit exaggerated. It works because it acknowledges the silliness of the situation, while still paying a compliment. The humor comes from the clever wordplay and the confidence it requires to pull it off.

Both of these examples rely on humor to diffuse the awkwardness of starting a conversation. They don't demand a serious response and invite the other person to engage in a light-hearted exchange.

Another Ukrainian Example:

- **Ти як сонце, бо освітлюєш мій день.**
  (You're like the sun, because you brighten my day.)

  This line is a bit more sincere and romantic. It doesn't rely on humor, but instead, it uses a metaphor to pay a heartfelt compliment. It's charming because it flatters the person in a thoughtful way.

These examples show that whether the line is humorous or sincere, it works because it doesn't take itself too seriously, and it creates an opportunity for a natural conversation.

Key Elements of an Effective Pickup Line

Now that we've looked at what makes pickup lines work, let's break down the essential elements of an effective pickup line. Understanding these elements will help you craft your own lines and use them confidently in various situations.

1. Humor

   Humor is one of the most powerful tools in flirting. A playful joke or a witty line can help break the ice and make the other person feel comfortable. A funny pickup line doesn't have to be a laugh-out-loud joke, but it should bring a smile to the other person's face. It shows that you don't take yourself too seriously and are confident enough to be playful. For example:

   - **Ти Wi-Fi? Бо я відчуваю зв'язок.**
     (Are you wifi? Because I feel a connection.)

   This line works because it's light-hearted and modern, referencing technology in a humorous way to make the other person smile.

2. Compliments

   Compliments are an easy way to show admiration, but they need to be sincere and not too over the top. The key is to keep the compliment light and avoid putting too much pressure on the interaction. For example:

- **У тебе чарівна усмішка.**
  (You have a lovely smile.)

This is a classic compliment that is simple, sincere, and flattering without being too intense.

3. Confidence

No matter how clever or well-crafted a pickup line is, it won't work if you don't deliver it with confidence. When you say a line, it's important to maintain eye contact, smile, and use a tone that feels natural. Confidence shows that you're comfortable with yourself and with the situation, which is an attractive quality in any culture.

4. Cultural Awareness

As we discussed earlier, knowing when and where to use a pickup line is crucial. What might work in a casual, playful setting could fall flat or even offend in a more formal or conservative context. Being aware of cultural norms and adjusting your approach accordingly is essential to successful flirting. For example, in a more reserved environment, you might opt for something simple and respectful like:

- **Приємно познайомитися. Мені подобається твій стиль.**
  (It's a pleasure to meet you. I love your style.)

This line is subtle but flattering and works well in more conservative or formal settings.

CATEGORIES OF PICKUP LINES

When it comes to flirting, not all pickup lines are created equal. Depending on the context, the person you're speaking to, and the mood of the situation, different types of pickup lines will be more effective. In Ukrainian culture, as in any culture, the key is to know when to be playful, when to embrace the cheesiness, and when to be sincere and romantic. In this section, we'll explore three types of pickup lines—humorous, cheesy, and romantic—and discuss how to use them effectively in different contexts. Along the way, we'll provide examples of each category to help you understand how these lines work.

Humorous Pickup Lines: Breaking the Ice with Laughter

Humor is a universal way to break the ice and make someone feel at ease. In Ukrainian culture, humor is often used to lighten the mood and show that you're not taking yourself too seriously. Humorous pickup lines are great for relaxed, casual settings where you want to open up a playful conversation. These lines typically work best when both people are in a light-hearted mood, such as at a party, a bar, or even on a casual date.

The key to a successful humorous pickup line is not just the words themselves but the delivery. A playful tone, a confident smile, and good timing can turn a simple joke into a memorable moment.

Examples:

- **Ти віриш у кохання з першого погляду, чи мені пройти повз ще раз?**
  (Do you believe in love at first sight, or should I walk by again?)

  This line plays on the classic "love at first sight" trope but adds humor by suggesting the person may need to walk by again for the effect to take hold. It's light, clever, and doesn't take the situation too seriously, making it perfect for a casual setting.

- **Ти Wi-Fi? Бо я відчуваю зв'язок.**
  (Are you wifi? Because I feel a connection.)

  This modern, tech-inspired pickup line is playful and relevant in today's world. It works well in informal environments, like a bar or a café, where a little humor can make the conversation more fun.

Why They Work:

Humorous pickup lines are designed to make the other person smile or laugh, which immediately sets a positive tone. In Ukrainian culture, where humor is often used to ease social interactions, these lines show that you're confident, easygoing, and willing to make the conversation enjoyable.

Cheesy Pickup Lines: Embracing the Corniness

Cheesy pickup lines, often referred to as "*банальні*" or "*солодкі*" in Ukrainian, can be surprisingly effective when used in the right context. What makes a cheesy line work is the acknowledgment that it's over-the-top and a little ridiculous—this self-awareness often makes the line endearing rather than off-putting. In Ukrainian culture, where charm and wit are appreciated, using a cheesy line with confidence can turn an awkward moment into a playful one.

These lines are great for light-hearted situations where both parties are in the mood for a bit of fun. They are often used in social environments like bars, clubs, or casual gatherings, where a bit of humor and charm can go a long way.

Examples:

- **У тебе є карта? Бо я загубився в твоїх очах.**
  (Do you have a map? Because I'm lost in your eyes.)

  This line is undeniably cheesy, but that's what makes it charming. It's exaggerated and dramatic, but it works because it doesn't take itself seriously.

- **Ти камера? Бо щоразу, коли я бачу тебе, я усміхаюся.**
  (Are you a camera? Because every time I see you, I smile.)

  Another classic cheesy line, this one uses a playful metaphor to flatter the person. It's corny, but it shows that you're comfortable being a little over-the-top in the name of fun.

Why They Work:

Cheesy pickup lines work when the person delivering them does so with confidence and a sense of humor. They're effective because they break down barriers by making both parties acknowledge the silliness of the line, creating a shared moment of light-heartedness. In Ukrainian culture, where humor and charm are valued in flirting, these lines can create a memorable and playful connection.

Romantic Pickup Lines: Sincere and Heartfelt Flirting

Romantic pickup lines are more direct and should be used when the mood feels right—when the conversation has moved beyond casual flirting and you want to express deeper admiration. These lines work well in more intimate settings, such as a one-on-one date, a quiet café, or during a meaningful conversation.

In Ukrainian culture, where passion and romance are often celebrated, a well-timed romantic line can create a powerful connection. However, it's important to make sure the line feels genuine and that the moment is appropriate. Using a romantic line too soon or in a setting that doesn't call for it can come off as awkward or insincere.

Examples:

- **Ти саме те, що я шукав, навіть не знаючи про це.**
  (You're exactly what I was looking for without knowing it.)

  This line is simple but deeply romantic. It works because it's not overly dramatic, yet it conveys a strong sense of admiration and attraction. It's perfect for a quiet, intimate moment when the connection feels real.

- **Якби я був художником, я б малював тебе все життя.**
  (If I were a painter, I'd paint you for life.)

  This line is more poetic and works in a context where the mood is already romantic. It's ideal for someone who appreciates creativity and sentimentality, and it conveys a deep sense of admiration in a unique way.

Why They Work:

Romantic pickup lines work when they're used in the right moment and delivered with sincerity. They show that you're willing to move beyond playful flirting and express genuine interest. In Ukrainian culture, where romance and passion are often embraced, a heartfelt line can help build a deeper connection when the time is right.

When to Use Each Type of Pickup Line

The key to using pickup lines successfully is knowing when and where to use each type. In general:

- **Humorous pickup lines** are best for breaking the ice in casual, relaxed environments. They work well when you want to make someone laugh and start a light-hearted conversation.

- **Cheesy pickup lines** are great for social situations where the goal is to have fun and not take the interaction too seriously. They work well when both people are in the mood for a bit of playful banter.

- **Romantic pickup lines** should be saved for more intimate or meaningful moments, where you want to express genuine admiration or deepen the connection.

By understanding the context and adjusting your approach accordingly, you can use pickup lines to create a connection that feels natural and engaging.

ADAPTING PICKUP LINES TO DIFFERENT ENVIRONMENTS

Flirting isn't a one-size-fits-all approach. The success of a pickup line often depends on the environment in which it's used. Different settings require different tones, levels of formality, and delivery styles. What works at a casual café may not be as effective in a lively nightclub, and flirting online calls for an entirely different approach. Adapting your pickup lines to fit the context ensures that you not only make a good impression but also connect in a way that feels natural and appropriate for the moment.

In this section, we'll focus on three common flirting environments—cafés or restaurants, bars or nightclubs, and online dating or social media—and provide examples of pickup lines that fit each setting. We'll also discuss how to adjust your delivery depending on the formality and tone of the environment.

Cafés or Restaurants: Casual and Comfortable

Cafés and restaurants offer a more relaxed and intimate setting, making them ideal for casual and friendly pickup lines. Here, people are usually focused on enjoying their coffee or meal, so the key is to approach in a way that doesn't feel intrusive. A light, respectful, and sincere line works well in this environment, as it complements the laid-back atmosphere.

Tone and Delivery:

In a café or restaurant, your tone should be warm and approachable. It's important to be respectful of the person's space, especially if they're alone or with friends. A soft smile, eye contact, and a gentle tone are ideal for making your approach feel natural.

Examples:

- **Ти завжди п'єш каву наодинці, чи я можу приєднатися?**
  (Do you always drink coffee alone, or can I join you?)

  This line is simple, non-intrusive, and provides a gentle invitation to continue the conversation. It fits well with the casual vibe of a café, where people often come to relax and enjoy their coffee.

- **Ти здаєшся такою ж солодкою, як десерт, який я збираюся замовити.**
  (You seem as sweet as the dessert I'm about to order.)

  This playful line incorporates the setting into the compliment. It's light-hearted and flirty without being overly bold, making it a great fit for a café or restaurant where the mood is casual and comfortable.

Why It Works:

In these relaxed settings, a pickup line that is sincere and low-pressure works best. People often come to cafés or restaurants to unwind, so a friendly and respectful approach helps create a positive connection without being too forward.

Bars or Nightclubs: Playful and Confident

Bars and nightclubs are much more energetic environments, which means the tone of your pickup line can be bolder and more playful. In these settings, people are usually more open to socializing, so you have more room to be confident and flirty. Humor and charm go a long way in a bar or nightclub, where the lively atmosphere encourages spontaneity and fun.

Tone and Delivery:

In a bar or nightclub, you can afford to be more direct and playful. Eye contact, a confident posture, and a lively tone will help your line land well in this environment. The key is to match the energy of the space—people are there to have fun, so your pickup line should reflect that.

Examples:

- **Хочеш потанцювати чи спочатку поспілкуємося?**
  (Would you like to dance, or would you prefer to chat first?)

  This line is great for a nightclub, where dancing is often a focal point. It's playful and gives the other person a choice, which keeps the tone light and fun without coming on too strong.

- **DJ щойно поставив нашу пісню. Йдемо?**
  (The DJ just played our song. Shall we go?)

  This line assumes a playful familiarity, which works well in the high-energy atmosphere of a bar or nightclub. It's bold and fun, perfect for someone who's confident and in tune with the lively environment.

Why It Works:

Bars and nightclubs are all about energy and connection. Pickup lines in these settings can afford to be more direct and playful because people are generally more open to social interaction. A bold approach that matches the lively atmosphere can create an instant connection.

Online Dating or Social Media: Thoughtful and Creative

Online dating and social media present a different kind of environment for pickup lines. Because there's no face-to-face interaction initially, the tone of your message needs to be more thoughtful and creative to stand out. The key to success in this space is crafting a line that shows genuine interest while also maintaining a light, approachable tone. Since you're not relying on body language or immediate reactions, your words need to do all the work.

Tone and Delivery:

When flirting online, your tone should be friendly, engaging, and a bit more deliberate. You can afford to be creative, but avoid coming on too strong. Personalization is key—referencing something from the person's profile, such as a hobby or interest, can make your approach feel more genuine.

Examples:

- **Провести вправо на тобі було найрозумнішим, що я зробив сьогодні.**
  (Swiping right on you was the smartest thing I did today.)

  This line is playful and shows that you're confident, while also acknowledging the shared experience of using a dating app. It's light and fun, making it a great way to start a conversation.

- **Ти не проти, якщо я перегляну твої фото?**
  (Do you mind if I walk you through your photos?)

  This is a clever way of referencing social media photos while subtly flirting. It's light-hearted and creative, which helps it stand out in an online setting where many messages can feel generic.

Why It Works:

In the online space, where direct interaction is limited, personalized pickup lines that show you've taken the time to read someone's profile or look at their interests can be very effective. The right balance of creativity and sincerity helps your message rise above the rest, making it more likely to lead to a meaningful conversation.

Formality and Tone: Adjusting Based on the Environment

One of the most important aspects of adapting pickup lines to different environments is understanding the level of formality and tone that fits the setting. Here's a quick guide:

- **Cafés or Restaurants:**
  Tone: Casual, friendly, warm

  These settings call for relaxed lines that show respect and genuine interest without being overly bold. People are often there to unwind, so a light and sincere approach works best.

- **Bars or Nightclubs:**
  Tone: Playful, confident, bold

  In a lively environment like a bar or nightclub, your lines can be more direct and energetic. Confidence is key here, as the social atmosphere encourages more daring interactions.

- **Online Dating or Social Media:**
  Tone: Creative, thoughtful, light

  Since online flirting relies solely on words, a personalized and creative approach helps you stand out. Playful lines with a touch of sincerity show that you've put effort into your message, making it more likely to grab attention.

Matching Your Lines to the Setting

Adapting your pickup lines to different environments ensures that your approach feels appropriate and natural. Whether you're in a cozy café, a lively nightclub, or on a dating app, tailoring your tone and delivery to fit the setting helps create a connection that feels right for the moment. By adjusting your lines based on the formality and energy of the environment, you increase your chances of making a memorable impression.

THE DOS AND DON'TS OF USING PICKUP LINES

Pickup lines can be a fun, effective way to break the ice and show interest in someone, but like any social interaction, there's an art to knowing when and where to use them. The key to successful flirting is understanding the context, reading the mood, and using pickup lines in a way that feels natural and respectful. A great line at the wrong time or in the wrong environment can feel awkward or even make the other person uncomfortable.

In this section, we'll cover the dos and don'ts of using pickup lines, exploring how cultural context, setting, and social cues can impact the success of a line. We'll also look at situations where pickup lines should be avoided altogether, and provide tips on how to gauge the other person's interest before proceeding.

The Dos: When and How to Use Pickup Lines Successfully

Knowing when to use a pickup line is just as important as choosing the right line itself. Pickup lines work best in situations where the atmosphere is relaxed, social, and light-hearted. Here are some key dos to keep in mind when deciding whether to use a pickup line:

1. **Do Use Pickup Lines in Casual, Social Settings**

   Environments like bars, cafés, parties, or social gatherings are generally great places to try out pickup lines. People are often there to relax and socialize, making them more open to playful interactions. In these settings, a friendly, respectful line can be an enjoyable way to start a conversation.

   Example:

   - At a party, a playful line like *"Ти Wi-Fi? Бо я відчуваю зв'язок."* (Are you wifi? Because I feel a connection.) can make someone smile and open the door to further conversation.

2. **Do Consider the Cultural Context**

   In Ukrainian culture, flirtation is often sincere and heartfelt, but it's important to adjust your approach depending on the region or setting. For example, in larger cities like Kyiv, flirting might be more open and playful, while in smaller towns or traditional areas, it tends to be more reserved and subtle. Being aware of these cultural nuances can help you connect with others in a thoughtful and respectful manner.

   Tip:

   - In more conservative environments, start with a simple compliment like *"У тебе чарівна усмішка."* (You have a lovely smile.) to gauge the other person's comfort level.

3. **Do Match the Mood of the Moment**

   The success of a pickup line often depends on the energy and mood of the situation. If the environment feels upbeat and lively, a more playful line may work well. If the setting is quieter or more intimate, consider a line that's subtle and sincere.

   Example:

   - In a relaxed café setting, a line like *"Ти завжди п'єш каву наодинці, чи я можу приєднатися?"* (Do you always drink coffee alone, or can I join you?) is gentle and respectful, aligning with the more low-key atmosphere.

4. **Do Pay Attention to Body Language and Social Cues**

   Pickup lines are best received when the other person seems open to interaction. Look for positive body language, such as open posture, eye contact, or a friendly smile. If the person seems interested, a well-timed pickup line can help break the ice.

   Tip:

   - If they respond with a smile or mirror your posture, it's usually a sign that they're open to engaging in conversation.

The Don'ts: When Pickup Lines Can Backfire

Just as important as knowing when to use a pickup line is knowing when not to. Using a line in the wrong context or setting can make the interaction feel forced or uncomfortable. Here are some don'ts to consider:

1. **Don't Use Pickup Lines in Formal or Professional Settings**

   In professional or formal environments, such as workplaces, conferences, or academic settings, it's best to avoid pickup lines altogether. These settings require a level of professionalism that doesn't usually lend itself to flirting. Even a well-meaning line can feel out of place or inappropriate.

   Example:

   - At a work event, it's better to stick to neutral compliments like *"Приємно познайомитися"* (It's a pleasure to meet you) and focus on friendly conversation rather than flirtation.

2. **Don't Force a Line if the Person Isn't Receptive**

   Flirting should feel natural, and if the other person isn't showing signs of interest, it's important to respect their space. Avoid using pickup lines if the person seems distracted, closed-off, or uninterested. If they aren't making eye contact or giving short, polite responses, it may be best to simply move on.

Tip:

- If someone is using closed body language (like crossed arms or looking away frequently), this is usually a sign they aren't open to further engagement.

3. Don't Use Pickup Lines That Are Too Forward or Inappropriate for the Setting

Some lines may feel appropriate in a lively bar or party but come off as overly bold in other situations. For example, a line like *"Ти неймовірно гарний/красива, як це ти сидиш тут сам/сима?"* (You're incredibly handsome/beautiful, how are you sitting here alone?) may work well in a fun, social setting, but could feel too intense in a quieter or more public place.

Tip:

- If you're unsure whether a line is too forward, opt for something simple and sincere. Testing the waters with a casual comment or light compliment can help you gauge the other person's response.

4. Don't Ignore the Importance of Timing

   Timing is everything when it comes to delivering a pickup line. Using a line too early in the interaction can feel abrupt, while waiting too long may make it lose impact. Find a natural moment to introduce your line, ideally after some initial eye contact or light conversation.

   Example:

   - If you're in a café, try waiting until you've made eye contact a couple of times before approaching with a line like *"Здається, у нас обох гарний смак щодо вибору кафе."* (Looks like we both have good taste in café spots.)

Reading Social Cues: Knowing When to Continue or Step Back

One of the most important skills in flirting is being able to read social cues. Recognizing when someone is interested or uninterested allows you to adjust your approach and avoid awkward situations. Here are a few tips on reading and responding to social cues:

- **Positive Cues:**

  Look for signs like consistent eye contact, leaning in, or mirroring your body language. These signals suggest that the other person is engaged and interested, and you can proceed with confidence.

- **Neutral or Uncertain Cues:**

  If the person is polite but not fully engaged—such as giving short answers or glancing around the room—consider adjusting your approach or focusing on friendly conversation before introducing a pickup line.

- **Negative Cues:**

  Signs like crossed arms, looking away, or checking their phone indicate that the person may not be interested. In this case, it's respectful to wrap up the conversation politely and give them space.

Example of Adjusting Based on Social Cues:

If you deliver a pickup line like *"Я не був/була готовий/готова побачити тебе й залишитися без слів."* (I wasn't ready to see you and be left speechless) and the other person smiles and responds warmly, continue with a follow-up question. However, if they only respond with a polite "thanks" and turn away, best to move on.

Knowing When to Use Pickup Lines Respectfully

The success of a pickup line depends on timing, setting, and your ability to read the other person's cues. In Ukrainian culture, where warmth and expressiveness are appreciated, a well-placed pickup line can create a fun, memorable moment. However, respect and attentiveness are key—being able to recognize when a line will be well-received versus when to hold back is what makes flirting feel natural and enjoyable.

PERSONALIZED PICKUP LINES BASED ON SHARED INTERESTS

Flirting is about connection, and one of the best ways to establish a connection is by showing genuine interest in what the other person enjoys. Personalized pickup lines tailored to someone's hobbies or passions can go beyond the surface level of standard compliments, demonstrating that you're paying attention to who they are as an individual. When you customize your approach based on shared interests, whether it's a love for books, music, or other hobbies, you make the conversation more meaningful and memorable.

In Ukrainian culture, where personal connections and relationships often take center stage, a personalized pickup line can signal that you're not just interested in a quick compliment but in forming a deeper bond. This section will guide you through how to tailor your pickup lines to fit specific interests and hobbies, with examples in both English and Ukrainian.

Why Personalized Pickup Lines Work

The beauty of personalized pickup lines lies in their ability to engage the other person on a deeper level. Instead of relying on generic compliments, you're showing that you've taken the time to notice something specific about them. Personalized lines can spark conversations that are richer and more engaging, as they allow the other person to talk about something they care about.

In addition, when a pickup line is based on a shared interest, it helps build rapport and trust more quickly. If both of you are passionate about music, art, sports, or travel, using that interest as a foundation can make the conversation flow naturally, as you both have a common ground to build on.

For Book Lovers: Flirting Through Literature

Books have a way of revealing a person's inner world, and if you meet someone who's a book lover, referencing literature in your pickup lines can create an instant connection. Whether you're discussing a favorite novel or playfully flirting with literary metaphors, this approach shows that you value intellect and creativity.

Examples:

- **Тобі подобаються книги? Бо кожна глава, яку я бачу в тобі, змушує мене хотіти читати більше.**
  (Do you like books? Because every chapter I see in you, I want to read more.)

  This line uses a playful metaphor to compliment the person while subtly referencing their love for literature. It works well because it's not too forward, and it connects to their intellectual side.

- **Якби ти був/була книгою, ти б став/стала бестселером.**
  (If you were a book, you'd be a bestseller.)

  This light-hearted compliment is both flattering and humorous, making it a great icebreaker for a conversation about books.

Why It Works:

Using book-related pickup lines creates an opportunity to discuss literature, and this can easily transition into a deeper conversation about favorite authors, genres, or novels. In Ukrainian culture, where storytelling and literature are highly appreciated, this kind of personalized line is sure to leave a lasting impression.

For Music Lovers: Tuning Into Romance

Music can be a powerful force that brings people together, and using pickup lines that reference a shared love for music can create a harmonious connection. Whether they play an instrument, sing, or are simply a music enthusiast, a well-timed music-themed pickup line can strike the right chord in your conversation.

Examples:

- **Ти музикант? Бо ти влучаєш у всі правильні ноти в моєму серці.**
  (Are you a musician? Because you're hitting all the right notes in my heart.)

  This line is playful and charming, and it works because it uses a music metaphor to deliver a heartfelt compliment without being too serious.

- **Якби наше життя було піснею, це була б найкраща мелодія, яку я коли-небудь чув/чула.**
  (If our life were a song, it would be the best melody I've ever heard.)

  This line is more romantic, evoking imagery of life as a melody. It's ideal for someone who appreciates deeper, more thoughtful compliments.

Why It Works:

Music-themed pickup lines work well because they tap into the emotional and expressive nature of music. Whether you're in a casual setting like a concert or just chatting about favorite bands, these lines help establish a connection that feels personal and meaningful. In Ukrainian culture, where music often plays a significant role in social gatherings, from traditional folk songs to modern pop, referencing this shared love for music can instantly create a connection.

For Art Lovers: A Creative Approach

If the person you're flirting with has a passion for the arts—whether it's painting, photography, or other creative pursuits—using pickup lines that speak to their artistic side can be a unique way to connect. Art-themed lines show that you appreciate beauty and creativity, making the conversation feel more inspired and thoughtful.

Examples:

- **Якби ти був/була твором мистецтва, ти б став/стала найціннішою картиною в музеї.**
  (If you were a work of art, you'd be the most valuable painting in the museum.)

  This line elevates the compliment by placing the person in the context of art, a metaphor that suggests admiration and appreciation.

- **Я не художник, але з тобою я міг/могла б створити шедевр.**
  (I'm not a painter, but with you, I could create a masterpiece.)

  This line is playful yet creative, appealing to the artistic nature of the person while delivering a romantic compliment.

Why It Works:

Art-themed pickup lines demonstrate that you can appreciate someone's creativity and the beauty they bring into the world. In Ukrainian culture, where the arts have a rich heritage, from iconic poets like Shevchenko to world-renowned composers like Lyatoshynsky, this approach adds a touch of sophistication to your flirting.

For Foodies: Flirting Over Flavor

Food is a universal love language, and if you're flirting with someone who's passionate about gastronomy, using pickup lines that reference food can add flavor to the conversation. Whether they love cooking or exploring new restaurants, these lines are sure to grab their attention.

Examples:

- **Ти кухар? Бо ти щойно додав/додала ідеальний штрих до мого дня.**
  (Are you a chef? Because you just added the perfect touch to my day.)

  This line is playful and flattering, making it ideal for someone who loves cooking or experimenting with food.

- **Ти здаєшся такою ж солодкою, як десерт, який я збираюся замовити.**
  (You seem as sweet as the dessert I'm about to order.)

  This line is light-hearted and works perfectly in a café or restaurant setting, connecting the compliment to the shared experience of enjoying food.

Why It Works:

Food-themed pickup lines are effective because they tap into a shared love for flavor, creativity, and shared meals. In Ukrainian culture, where food plays a central role in bringing people together, this kind of personalized line can set the stage for a fun and engaging conversation.

For Travelers: Exploring New Connections

If the person you're talking to loves to travel, referencing their adventurous spirit in a pickup line can instantly pique their interest. Travel-related lines show that you're open to exploring new experiences and cultures, which can be an attractive quality.

Examples:

- **Якби ти був/була місцем призначення, це було б те місце, куди я завжди хотів/хотіла б повертатися.**
  (If you were a destination, you'd be the place I'd always want to return to.)

  This romantic and adventurous line is perfect for someone who loves traveling and exploring the world.

- **Тобі подобається подорожувати? Бо я відчуваю, що ми збираємося вирушити у велику пригоду.**
  (Do you like traveling? Because I feel like we're about to embark on a great adventure.)

  This line is playful and references the excitement of starting a new journey, making it ideal for someone with a passion for travel.

Why It Works:

Travel-themed pickup lines work because they tap into the other person's sense of adventure and curiosity. They create the feeling of embarking on a journey together, which can be a powerful metaphor for flirting. In Ukrainian culture, where travel and exploration are often celebrated, these lines can lead to deeper conversations about shared experiences and dreams.

Making Flirting Personal

Personalized pickup lines are a great way to make flirting more meaningful and memorable. By tailoring your approach to the other person's interests, whether they're a book lover, music enthusiast, or foodie, you show that you're paying attention and that you care about what makes them unique. In Ukrainian culture, where personal connections and shared passions are highly valued, using customized lines that align with someone's hobbies or passions can help build a stronger, more authentic connection.

CHAPTER THREE:
FORMAL VS. INFORMAL FLIRTING

THE ROLE OF TONE: FORMAL VS. INFORMAL FLIRTING

Tone plays a significant role in communication, especially when it comes to flirting. In Ukrainian, the choice between formal and informal language can dramatically change the tone of your conversation. Using formal language shows respect and politeness, while informal language tends to be more relaxed and playful. Knowing when and how to switch between these tones can help you navigate various social situations with confidence.

In this section, we'll explore when to use formal language—particularly in more conservative or respectful settings—and when informal language is appropriate, such as in casual social environments like bars or online dating.

When to Use Formal Language in Flirting

In Ukrainian culture, formal language is often used in professional or traditional settings, or when addressing someone older or in a position of authority. Flirting in these situations requires a delicate balance of expressing interest while maintaining courtesy and respect. Using formal pronouns like "*Bu*" and polite phrases is essential to demonstrate respect and create a positive impression.

Here are some situations where formal language is more appropriate:

1. **When Meeting Someone for the First Time in a Professional or Conservative Environment**

   If you're meeting someone at a formal event, a workplace function, or in a setting where social norms require a more respectful approach, it's best to use formal language.

   - Example:

     - **У вас чарівна усмішка.**
       (You have a lovely smile.)

       This is a formal compliment that conveys admiration in a polite and respectful way. It's subtle enough for more formal settings without being too forward.

     - **Чи хотіли б ви якось піти зі мною на побачення?**
       (Would you like to go out with me sometime?)

       This phrase is polite and respectful, showing interest while using the formal tone appropriate for conservative environments.

2. **When Addressing Someone Older**

   In Ukrainian culture, addressing someone older than you with formal language is a sign of respect. Even in a romantic setting, the use of the formal "*Ви*" demonstrates politeness and consideration, showing that you value the person and their boundaries.

- Example:

  - **Приємно познайомитися. Що ви думаєте про цю вечірку?**
    (It's a pleasure to meet you. What do you think of this party?)

    This maintains a polite and formal tone but is still conversational. In a more traditional environment, this can be an excellent way to balance respect and flirting.

3. **When Flirting in a More Traditional Culture**

Some Ukrainians may value more traditional, respectful approaches to flirting. Using formal language can show that you're serious and considerate, especially when speaking to someone for the first time.

- Example:

  - **Ви дуже чарівна людина.**
    (I find you to be a very charming person.)

    This formal phrase expresses admiration in a respectful way and could work well in more conservative contexts.

When to Use Informal Language in Flirting

Informal language is much more common in casual social settings like bars, cafés, or even on dating apps. The tone here is relaxed, playful, and open. Informal flirting allows for more spontaneity and can create a sense of closeness faster than formal language.

Here are situations where informal language is appropriate:

1. **In Casual Social Settings (Bars, Parties, or Online Dating)**

    If you're at a bar, party, or using an online dating app, informal language is the way to go. People are more likely to be open and playful in these environments, so a more relaxed tone fits the mood.

    - Example:

        - **У тебе чарівна усмішка.**
          (You have a lovely smile.)

            In an informal setting, this compliment feels more direct and personal. It's perfect for situations where you want to make a connection without the formality of *"Ви"*.

        - **Хочеш якось піти зі мною на побачення?**
          (Do you want to go out with me sometime?)

            This version of the request is more casual and could be used when flirting at a party or on a dating app. It feels more spontaneous and relaxed than the formal alternative.

2. **When Flirting with People Around Your Age or Younger**

   When speaking to people your age or younger in Ukrainian culture, it's generally acceptable to use informal language, especially in casual or flirtatious contexts. Using "*ти*" instead of "*Ви*" helps create a more personal and relaxed connection.

   - Example:

     - **Тобі подобається це місце? Ми можемо піти в інше, якщо хочеш.**
       (Do you like this place? We can go somewhere else if you'd like.)

       This casual tone makes the conversation feel more friendly and approachable, helping to ease any tension and keep things lighthearted.

3. **Flirting in a Playful, Lighthearted Manner**

   Informal language is ideal for playful and teasing flirting in Ukrainian. It allows you to use humor to break the ice and make the interaction more engaging.

   - Example:

     - **Гей, ти не загубився/загубилася? Бо виглядаєш так, ніби повинен/повинна бути на небесах.**
       (Hey, are you lost? Because you look like someone who should be in heaven.)

       This line, though cheesy, works well in informal settings like cafés, bars, or parties. Delivered with humor, it can make for a memorable opening.

Switching Between Formal and Informal Language

In Ukrainian, it's essential to know when to switch between formal and informal language based on the setting and the person you're speaking to. You might start with formal language to show respect, especially in professional or traditional contexts, and transition to informal language as the interaction becomes more personal.

For example, if you're meeting someone at a formal event, you could begin with something like:

- **У вас чарівна усмішка.**
  (You have a lovely smile.)

  This respectful tone sets the stage for a polite conversation.

As the conversation progresses and you both become more familiar, you could transition to:

- **У тебе чарівна усмішка. Як це я раніше тебе не зустрів/зустріла?**
  (You have a lovely smile. How come I haven't met you before?)

  Switching to "*ти*" signals that the conversation has become more familiar and relaxed, helping to deepen the connection.

VOCABULARY FOR FORMAL VS. INFORMAL FLIRTING

When it comes to flirting in Ukrainian, choosing the right words for the right context can make all the difference. Language is not just about vocabulary; it's about setting the tone, matching the environment, and adapting to social expectations. In more formal settings, respectful and subtle expressions are key, while informal environments often allow for more playful and casual language.

In this section, we'll explore specific vocabulary and phrases suited to both formal and informal flirting contexts, giving you the tools to navigate a variety of social situations.

Formal Flirting: Politeness and Subtlety

In formal settings, such as a dinner party, professional event, or even a family gathering, using respectful language can help convey interest in a tasteful way. Ukrainian has many ways to show admiration politely, allowing you to express yourself while respecting social boundaries.

- **Polite Expressions and Respectful Titles:**

    - **Мені б дуже хотілося запросити вас на побачення.** *(I would love to invite you out.)*

        This phrasing is gentle and polite, expressing interest without sounding too forward.

- **Ви дуже цікава людина.**
  (You are a very interesting person.)

  This phrase is complimentary without feeling overly personal, making it suitable for first encounters.

- **Приємно познайомитися, пане/пані.**
  (It's a pleasure to meet you, sir/ma'am.)

  Adding a respectful title like "*пане*" or "*пані*" when addressing someone, especially in formal contexts or when speaking to an older person, demonstrates good manners and cultural awareness.

- **Softer Language Choices:**

In formal situations, language is often softened to create a respectful tone.

- **Чи хотіли б ви якось разом випити кави?**
  (Would you like to get coffee someday?)

  Using the conditional "*чи хотіли б ви*" instead of a direct "*хочете*" makes the invitation sound more tentative and respectful, showing sensitivity to the other person's comfort.

- **Я б хотів/хотіла краще вас пізнати.**
  (I'd like to get to know you better.)

  The phrasing "*я б хотів/хотіла*" softens the statement, making it more formal and respectful, which is ideal for such settings.

Informal Flirting: Playfulness and Confidence

In relaxed or social settings, such as bars, parties, or friendly gatherings, informal flirting allows for a lighter, more casual approach. Here, expressions of admiration can be bolder, playful, and even sprinkled with local slang, depending on the country or region.

- **Playful Phrases and Colloquial Terms:**

    - **Ти мені дуже подобаєшся.**
      (I really like you.)

      Short and sweet, this phrase conveys attraction in a direct way. In informal contexts, you can skip the polite form and go straight to expressing admiration.

    - **Може, вип'ємо щось разом?**
      (Shall we get a drink?)

      This casual invitation works well in social settings and can easily start a conversation without feeling too formal or structured.

    - **Ти неймовірний/неймовірна.**
      (You're amazing.)

      Simple yet effective, this line is a friendly compliment that's direct but not overly romantic, making it suitable for first interactions in casual settings.

- **Slang and Regional Variations:**

    Depending on the region in Ukraine, certain phrases or colloquialisms can add humor and familiarity to your flirting. Here are a few examples:

    - **Ти просто бомба.**
      ("You're amazing" or "You're awesome.")

        This modern slang phrase is widely understood and conveys enthusiasm in a playful way.

    - **Ти класний/класна.**
      ("You're cool.")

        A friendly compliment that's both light-hearted and flattering, often used in informal conversations.

    - **Ти просто топ.**
      ("You're the best.")

        This casual and trendy expression is popular among younger Ukrainians, making it perfect for informal social settings.

FLIRTING IN PROFESSIONAL VS. SOCIAL ENVIRONMENTS

Flirting is all about context—and in professional versus social settings, knowing how to adjust your approach is essential. In a semi-formal or professional setting, boundaries and respect play a significant role. Using subtle language and indirect compliments is often best to avoid overstepping, especially when interactions could impact professional relationships. Meanwhile, in a casual social setting, there's generally more flexibility for playful and lighthearted language.

In this section, we'll explore how to adjust your flirting style depending on the environment, offering tips and examples for keeping things respectful in professional settings and reading the room in social gatherings.

Flirting in Professional Settings: Politeness and Subtlety

Flirting in a professional setting—whether at a work event, conference, or even a shared workplace—calls for a more restrained, thoughtful approach. Respectful language and subtle expressions help ensure that your interest doesn't disrupt the professional atmosphere or create discomfort.

Using Subtle Compliments

When giving compliments in a professional environment, it's best to focus on qualities that reflect respect, such as the other person's insights, work ethic, or style. Avoid compliments on appearance, which can easily feel too personal, and instead aim for neutral phrasing.

Examples of Subtle, Polite Compliments:

- **Я захоплююся вашим професійним підходом; це дуже надихає.**
  (I admire your professional approach; it's very inspiring.)

- **Ви завжди маєте свій погляд на речі, який змушує задуматися.**
  (You always have a way of seeing things that really makes one think.)

These compliments convey admiration without crossing into personal territory, making them appropriate and respectful in a professional setting.

Neutral Language for Professional Settings

In professional environments, consider using indirect expressions of interest. For instance, instead of suggesting a personal outing right away, frame it as an opportunity to connect on a shared interest. This can keep the tone neutral while still giving you a chance to establish a rapport.

Polite, Indirect Invitations:

- **Якщо у вас буде час, я б із задоволенням послухав/послухала більше про ваш досвід у цій галузі. Хотіли б якось випити кави?**
  (If you have time, I'd love to hear more about your experience in this field. Would you like to have coffee sometime?)

- **Я багато дізнався/дізналася з цієї розмови. Якщо у вас буде час, я б із задоволенням продовжив/продовжила її.**
  (I've learned a lot from this conversation. If you have time sometime, I'd love to continue it.)

These invitations keep the conversation light and professional, allowing the other person to accept or decline comfortably.

Flirting in Social Settings: Reading the Room

Social environments, like parties, bars, or gatherings, generally allow for a more relaxed and playful approach. However, it's still essential to read the room to determine if the other person is open to flirting and to adjust your tone accordingly.

Gauging the Vibe in Social Gatherings

In a social setting, observe the atmosphere before starting a flirtatious conversation. For instance, at a casual dinner with friends, people may be more relaxed and open to playful banter. At a family gathering or formal event, however, a polite approach may be more suitable.

Using Playful Language in Social Settings

Once you've gauged that the setting is appropriate, consider using a more informal or lighthearted tone. In contrast to the professional approach, social settings allow for direct compliments and playful language that conveys interest clearly.

Examples of Playful, Lighthearted Compliments:

- У вас є енергія, яка наповнює кімнату світлом.
  (You have an energy that lights up the room.)

- У вас, здається, чудове почуття гумору. Хотіли б приєднатися до нашої розмови?
  (You seem to have a great sense of humor. Would you like to join our conversation?)

These compliments are direct yet friendly, making them well-suited to a casual social environment.

Adjusting Tone Based on Response

After delivering a compliment or expressing interest, observe the other person's reaction. If they respond positively, with open body language and engaged conversation, you may feel comfortable continuing with a playful tone. If they seem reserved or give short responses, a polite, less personal tone may be a better fit.

Role-Playing Exercise: Practicing Professional vs. Social Flirting

Now that you've seen examples of flirting language for both professional and social settings, try this role-playing exercise to practice adapting your tone and expressions based on different scenarios. Imagine each scenario, choose the best approach, and consider how you might respond based on the other person's cues.

Scenario 1: Work Conference

You're attending a professional conference, and you meet someone who shares similar interests. You'd like to show appreciation and establish a friendly connection without crossing professional boundaries.

Suggested Approach:

- **Polite Compliment:** Мені дуже сподобалися ваші ідеї. У вас дійсно унікальний погляд.
  (I've loved hearing your ideas. You have a truly unique perspective.)

- **Indirect Invitation:** Якщо у вас буде час, я б із задоволенням обговорив/обговорила цю тему детальніше.
  (If you ever have time, I'd love to talk more about this topic.)

Outcome:

This approach keeps the interaction professional while opening the door for future conversation. The indirect invitation respects their professional boundaries and lets them decide whether to connect further.

Scenario 2: Casual Bar with Friends

You're at a bar with friends, and someone catches your eye. The atmosphere is friendly and relaxed, so you decide to strike up a conversation with a playful approach.

Suggested Approach:

- Direct Compliment: У вас заразлива усмішка. Я не міг/могла не помітити.
  (You have a contagious smile. I couldn't help but notice.)

- Playful Invitation: Якщо ви не зайняті, хотіли б приєднатися до нас?
  (If you're not busy, would you like to join us?)

Outcome:

In this informal setting, a direct compliment and lighthearted invitation match the relaxed vibe of the bar. If they respond positively, you can continue with friendly conversation and playful banter.

Scenario 3: Formal Networking Event

You're at a formal networking event, and you meet someone with an impressive background. While you'd like to get to know them better, you're mindful of the professional setting.

Suggested Approach:

- **Subtle Praise:** Надихає слухати про ваші досягнення. Я дійсно захоплююся вашим підходом.
  (It's inspiring to hear about your achievements. I really admire your approach.)

- **Neutral Invitation:** Якщо ви колись захочете поділитися більше про свої проєкти, було б чудово продовжити розмову.
  (If you ever want to share more about your projects, it'd be great to continue the conversation.)

Outcome:

This approach shows admiration while keeping the conversation professional and respectful. The neutral invitation leaves space for a future interaction without implying romantic interest outright.

Bringing It All Together

Flirting in different environments requires situational awareness and the ability to adjust your language and tone to suit the setting. In professional environments, keep compliments subtle, indirect, and focused on qualities that demonstrate admiration and respect. In social settings, use friendly and direct language that matches the informal vibe, while still observing the other person's comfort level.

By practicing these distinctions, you'll gain confidence in knowing when to keep things light and when to be more formal, ensuring your interactions feel appropriate, comfortable, and enjoyable for both parties.

FORMAL AND INFORMAL FLIRTING DIALOGUES IN ACTION

Understanding the nuances of formal and informal flirting comes to life when you see it in action. In this section, we'll explore two sample dialogues that highlight the differences in flirting style depending on the setting. One dialogue takes place in a workplace or formal event, where subtlety and politeness are key. The other is set in a casual environment like a bar or café, where relaxed language and playful humor are more appropriate.

By analyzing these dialogues, you'll gain insight into why certain phrases, gestures, and language choices suit each context. This will help you become more adaptable in your own interactions, developing an awareness of how to engage comfortably and respectfully in various settings.

Formal Dialogue: Workplace Networking Event

Imagine you're at a professional networking event, where you've just met someone you find interesting. You're both mindful of keeping the tone polite and professional, so you approach the conversation with subtle compliments and reserved language.

Formal Dialogue Example:

You: Приємно познайомитися. Ваша презентація була справді надихаючою.
(It's a pleasure to meet you. Your presentation was truly inspiring.)

Them: Дякую, ви дуже люб'язні. Радію, що це було корисно.
(Thank you, you're very kind. I'm glad to know it was helpful.)

You: Я дуже захоплююся вашим підходом. У вас є унікальний спосіб бачити речі, який дійсно змушує задуматися.
(I really admire your perspective. You have a way of looking at things that truly invites reflection.)

Them: Ну, саме це і є найкращим у таких заходах, чи не так? Завжди є чому навчитися одне від одного.
(Well, that's the great thing about these events, right? There's always something to learn from others.)

You: Безсумнівно. Власне, я б із задоволенням продовжив/продовжила цю розмову якось, якщо у вас буде час.
(Absolutely. In fact, I'd love to continue this conversation sometime if you have time.)

Them: Звичайно. Можливо, хотіли б випити кави наступного тижня?
(Of course. Would you like to have a coffee next week?)

You: Мені б дуже хотілося. Було б приємно краще вас пізнати.
(I'd love to. It would be a pleasure to get to know you better.)

Analysis

This exchange is characterized by polite, respectful language that maintains a professional tone. Key elements include:

- **Formal Pronouns and Phrasing:** The use of "*ви*" instead of "*ти*" keeps the conversation formal and appropriate for a workplace or professional event. This shows respect for the other person's position and boundaries.

- **Subtle Compliments:** Phrases like "*я дуже захоплююся вашим підходом*" (I really admire your perspective) express appreciation without being too personal, making them perfect for formal occasions.

- **Polite Invitation:** Instead of suggesting an informal meetup, the invitation is phrased as "*я б із задоволенням продовжив/продовжила цю розмову якось*" (I'd love to continue this conversation sometime), which keeps the tone professional and considerate of the other person's comfort.

This approach allows the conversation to flow naturally while maintaining professionalism and respect, helping build rapport without crossing any boundaries.

Informal Dialogue: Bar or Café

Now imagine you're in a relaxed setting like a bar or café, where the atmosphere is friendly, and people are more open to casual conversation. Here, you can be more direct and playful with your language, showing interest with humor and informal phrasing.

Informal Dialogue Example:

You: Привіт, як справи? Не міг/могла не помітити твоєї усмішки — вона просто заразлива.
(Hi, how's it going? I couldn't help but notice your smile; it's contagious.)

Them: Дякую, це дуже мило. Тепер я усміхаюся ще більше.
(Thank you, that's a nice comment. It made me smile even more.)

You: Ти часто приходиш сюди, чи сьогодні мені просто пощастило?
(Do you come here often, or am I just lucky today?)

Them: Я іноді сюди заходжу. А ти?
(I come here from time to time. And you?)

You: Це моє улюблене місце, щоб розслабитися після роботи. Хоча сьогодні, здається, я знайшов/знайшла щось краще за каву.
(It's my favorite place to unwind after work. Though today, I think I found something even better than the coffee.)

Them: О, справді? Ну, думаю, нам варто це відсвяткувати.
(Oh, really? Well, I guess we should toast to that.)

You: Однозначно. Хочеш скласти мені компанію?
(Definitely. Would you like to join me?)

Analysis

In this relaxed, social context, the language is informal and playful, using "*ти*" and casual expressions to create a friendly and approachable atmosphere. Key elements include:

- **Direct Compliments:** Phrases like "*Не міг/могла не помітити твоєї усмішки — вона просто заразлива*" (I couldn't help but notice your smile — it's contagious) immediately draw attention in a positive way, showing interest without being overly serious.

- **Playful Questions:** "*Ти часто приходиш сюди, чи сьогодні мені просто пощастило?*" (Do you come here often, or am I just lucky today?) adds humor and invites a lighthearted exchange.

- **Relaxed Tone:** The use of "*ти*" and casual phrasing fits the informal setting, allowing the conversation to feel natural and unrestrained.

In a casual setting, this approach fosters openness and encourages a positive response. By mixing compliments, playful questions, and a friendly tone, you can create a comfortable and engaging interaction.

Why Each Approach Works

Each dialogue is effective because it respects the boundaries of its setting:

1. **In Formal Settings:**

    - The formal dialogue maintains professionalism with subtle compliments, respectful pronouns, and polite invitations. These choices help avoid crossing personal boundaries while still showing genuine interest.

2. **In Informal Settings:**

    - The informal dialogue uses playful language, direct compliments, and casual phrasing, which suit a relaxed atmosphere. This approach makes it easy to establish a friendly connection and build rapport quickly.

Understanding how to adapt your language based on the setting enables you to approach flirting with confidence, whether you're at a networking event or a café. By paying attention to the tone, vocabulary, and structure of each exchange, you'll become more skilled at managing boundaries, allowing each interaction to feel both natural and respectful.

PRACTICE EXERCISES: TESTING FORMAL VS. INFORMAL FLIRTING SKILLS

Developing the ability to switch between formal and informal flirting styles is key to feeling confident in different social situations. These exercises are designed to help you practice choosing the right tone and language for various scenarios, helping you fine-tune your skills for any setting. You'll get a chance to pick or create suitable lines based on the context, followed by self-reflection prompts to help you consider your natural flirting style and how it might adapt according to cultural and situational cues.

Feel free to have fun with these exercises, as they're here to build your comfort and intuition for adapting your flirting style to suit formal and informal situations.

SCENARIO-BASED EXERCISES

Scenario 1: Meeting Someone at a Professional Conference

You're attending a professional conference where you meet someone who shares similar interests. You'd like to express admiration, but you want to keep things respectful due to the professional environment. We have three options. Choose the one that best matches a formal setting, and think about why it might be more appropriate than the others.

1. **Приємно познайомитися. Ваша презентація була справді надихаючою.**
   (It's a pleasure to meet you. Your presentation was truly inspiring.)

2. **Привіт, ви часто відвідуєте такі заходи? Приємно бачити знайоме обличчя.**
   (Hi, do you come to these events often? Nice to see a familiar face.)

3. **Мені дуже подобається ваш стиль. Хотіли б поспілкуватися після конференції?**
   (I really like your style. Would you like to chat more after the conference?)

Answer and Analysis:

The best choice is Option 1. This line keeps the tone polite and respectful, which suits a formal setting like a conference. It includes a compliment but remains professional, which is essential for maintaining boundaries in a workplace context.

Scenario 2: Casual Meetup at a Café

You're at a local café when you notice someone interesting sitting nearby. The setting is relaxed, and you have an opportunity to be more open and casual. Choose the line that best matches the informal vibe, and consider why this might feel more natural than a formal approach.

1. **Приємно познайомитися. Мені дуже подобається атмосфера тут.**
   (It's a pleasure to meet you. I've been enjoying the atmosphere here.)

2. **Привіт, ви часто приходите до цього кафе? Виглядає як ідеальне місце для відпочинку.**
   (Hi, do you come to this café often? It seems like the perfect spot to unwind.)

3. **Я б із задоволенням запросив/запросила вас на каву якось. Приємно познайомитися з кимось новим.**
   (I'd love to invite you for coffee sometime. It's great to meet someone new.)

Answer and Analysis:

Option 2 is the best choice here. The casual question, *"Ви часто приходите до цього кафе?"* (Do you come to this café often?), fits a relaxed environment like a café and is a friendly, non-intrusive way to start a conversation.

Scenario 3: Formal Event or Family Gathering

Imagine you're at a formal family gathering or social event where people are expected to maintain a certain level of decorum. You meet someone new, and while you'd like to show interest, you want to keep things polite. Choose the line that would best suit this setting.

1. **Мені приємно познайомитися з вами. Чи хотіли б ви продовжити цю розмову якось пізніше?**
   (I'm glad to meet you. Would you like to continue this conversation sometime?)

2. **Привіт, у вас є енергія, яка дійсно наповнює кімнату світлом.**
   (Hi, you have an energy that really lights up the room.)

3. **Мені подобається знайомитися з новими людьми. Хотіли б якось піти на прогулянку?**
   (I love meeting new people. Would you like to go out sometime?)

Answer and Analysis:

Option 1 is the best choice for a formal event. This line maintains respect and politeness without suggesting too much personal interest right away. The use of the formal pronoun "*ви*" and courteous phrasing is ideal for a family-oriented or formal setting, ensuring your words are appropriate and well-received.

Create Your Own Responses

Now that you've had some practice, try creating your own responses for different scenarios. Use the cues provided to guide your choice of tone and vocabulary.

1. **Scenario:** You're introduced to someone interesting at a work networking event. How would you express interest while remaining professional?

    Your Answer: "_____
    _____"

2. **Scenario:** You're at a friend's party and notice someone you'd like to get to know better. What informal line would you use to break the ice?

    Your Answer: "_____
    _____"

3. **Scenario:** You're at a cultural event, such as a museum exhibit, and meet someone who shares your interests. How would you show interest in a way that's respectful but friendly?

    Your Answer: "_____
    _____"

By creating responses based on these scenarios, you'll build your adaptability in various settings, helping you refine both your formal and informal flirting skills.

Self-Reflection Prompts

To better understand your natural flirting style and how you might adjust it based on cultural or situational cues, take a moment to reflect on these questions. This will help you identify your comfort zone and areas where you might want to adapt.

1. What's your usual approach to flirting?

    - Do you naturally lean toward a formal or informal style? Do you tend to use humor, direct compliments, or more subtle expressions of interest?

2. How do you adjust your style in different settings?

    - Think about past situations. How have you adapted your approach in professional versus social environments? Were there times when you shifted from formal to informal, or vice versa, based on the other person's reactions?

3. What cultural cues do you find most useful?

    - Consider what cultural or social cues you've noticed in various settings. Do you pay attention to body language, the use of formal versus informal language, or how others react to your tone? Identifying these cues can help you become more attuned to adjusting your style as needed.

By engaging in these reflection prompts, you'll gain valuable insights into how you naturally approach flirting and where you can enhance your adaptability. Being mindful of these nuances can help you build more comfortable and authentic connections, whether you're in a formal or informal setting.

CHAPTER FOUR:
DATING VOCABULARY & USEFUL PHRASES

ESSENTIAL VOCABULARY FOR DATING AND RELATIONSHIPS

When it comes to dating, having a strong foundation in the vocabulary of relationships can make all the difference. Whether you're just beginning to know someone or progressing toward a deeper connection, understanding the right words and phrases in Ukrainian can help you navigate each stage confidently and express your feelings clearly. In this section, we'll introduce essential vocabulary related to dating and relationships, covering terms for expressing attraction, describing different relationship stages, and sharing emotions. By learning these terms, you'll be better equipped to connect and communicate in a meaningful way with a potential partner.

Key Terms for Dating and Relationships

Let's begin with the basics. Here are some foundational words you'll encounter when talking about dating and relationships in Ukrainian:

- **Побачення – Date**
  (Example: *Хотіли б піти зі мною на побачення?* – *Would you like to go on a date with me?*)

- **Партнер/партнерка – Partner**
  (Example: *Вона моя партнерка.* – *She is my partner.*)

- **Хлопець/дівчина – Boyfriend/Girlfriend**
  (Example: Він мій хлопець. – He is my boyfriend.)

- **Відносини – Relationship**
  (Example: У нас чудові відносини. – We have a great relationship.)

These terms are essential for referring to your date or your partner and can also help you clarify the status of your relationship.

Stages of a Relationship

As relationships progress, so does the language used to describe each stage. Here's a list of useful vocabulary that will help you express where you are in a relationship and how things are developing:

- **Зустрічати, знайомитися – To meet, to get to know**
  (Example: Я б дуже хотів/хотіла краще тебе пізнати. – I would love to get to know you better.)

- **Ходити разом – To go out together**
  (Example: Ми ходимо разом. – We are going out together.)

- **Серйозні відносини – Serious relationship**
  (Example: Ми хочемо мати серйозні відносини. – We want to have a serious relationship.)

- **Зобов'язання, заручини – Commitment, engagement**
  (Example: Ми заручені. – We are engaged.)

- **Шлюб – Marriage**
  (Example: Ми готуємося до шлюбу. – We are getting ready for marriage.)

Each of these terms helps describe the progression of a relationship, from the initial stages of meeting and dating to the commitment and marriage phase. Knowing these words can help you articulate what you're looking for or understand what your partner envisions.

Expressing Emotions and Attraction

Expressing emotions is a core part of any relationship. These words and phrases will help you convey how you feel about someone in Ukrainian, whether it's a simple expression of interest or something deeper:

- **Ти мені подобаєшся – I like you**
  (Example: Ти мені дуже подобаєшся. – I like you a lot.)

- **Я закоханий/закохана – I'm in love**
  (Example: Я закоханий/закохана в тебе. – I'm in love with you.)

- **Привабливість – Attraction**
  (Example: Між нами сильна привабливість. – There's a lot of attraction between us.)

- **Почуття – Feelings**
  (Example: Мої почуття до тебе дуже сильні. – My feelings for you are strong.)

- **Підтримка – Support**
  (Example: Ти завжди маєш мою підтримку. – You always have my support.)

These words allow you to express a range of feelings, from initial attraction to deep love and support, helping to create a more intimate connection with your partner.

COMPLIMENTING YOUR DATE: PHRASES TO MAKE AN IMPRESSION

Compliments are a powerful way to make someone feel valued, appreciated, and special. In Ukrainian culture, compliments are often used to convey admiration and interest, but it's essential to deliver them naturally and respectfully. This section introduces key phrases for complimenting appearance and personality, along with tips on when and how to use them to create a positive, memorable impression on your date.

Compliments About Appearance

When complimenting appearance, a few words can go a long way in making someone feel noticed and appreciated. Here are some useful phrases that highlight different aspects of physical appearance:

- **Ти виглядаєш неймовірно** – You look amazing
  (*Example:* Ти виглядаєш неймовірно сьогодні ввечері. – You look amazing tonight.)

- **У тебе чарівна усмішка** – You have a lovely smile
  (*Example:* У тебе чарівна усмішка, яка наповнює кімнату світлом. – You have a lovely smile that lights up the room.)

- **Ти дуже гарний/красива** – You're very handsome/beautiful
  (*Example:* Ти дуже гарний/красива; важко цього не помітити. – You're very handsome/beautiful; it's hard not to notice.)

- **У тебе красиві очі** – Your eyes are beautiful
  (*Example: Я не можу втриматися, у тебе красиві очі.* – *I can't help it; your eyes are beautiful.*)

These compliments focus on specific features, making them feel more personal and genuine. However, keep in mind that a little goes a long way—rather than piling on compliments, choose one or two that feel natural and well-timed to keep the interaction comfortable.

Compliments About Personality

Beyond appearance, complimenting someone's personality can be even more meaningful. These compliments express admiration for qualities that make your date unique and can lead to deeper, more genuine connections.

- **Мені подобається твоє почуття гумору** – I love your sense of humor
  (*Example: Мені подобається твоє почуття гумору; ти завжди змушуєш мене сміятися.* – *I love your sense of humor; you always manage to make me laugh.*)

- **Ти дуже цікавий/цікава** – You're very interesting
  (*Example: Ти дуже цікавий/цікава; щоразу, коли ми розмовляємо, я дізнаюся щось нове.* – *You're very interesting; every time we talk, I learn something new.*)

- **У тебе особлива енергія** – You have a special energy
  (*Example: У тебе особлива енергія, яка робить спілкування з тобою легким.* – *You have a special energy that makes it easy to be around you.*)

- **Ти мене надихаєш** – You inspire me
  (Example: Ти надихаєш мене бути кращим/кращою кожного дня. – You inspire me to be better every day.)

Personality-focused compliments go beyond the surface and show that you appreciate your date for who they truly are. Compliments like these are ideal for moments when you've gotten to know each other a bit, as they can foster a sense of closeness and mutual respect.

Tips for Giving Compliments Naturally and Respectfully

While compliments can enhance any date, knowing how to give them naturally is essential. Here are some tips for delivering compliments with authenticity and respect:

1. Be Specific

   - Rather than a generic compliment, choose something specific you genuinely admire. For example, instead of just saying *"Мені подобається твоя усмішка"* (I like your smile), say *"У тебе чарівна усмішка"* (you have a lovely smile), which feels more genuine.

2. Read the Room

   - Pay attention to your date's reactions and body language. If they respond warmly, they're likely comfortable with the compliment. If they seem shy or brush it off, ease back on compliments to avoid making them uncomfortable.

3. Use Compliments Sparingly

    - A few well-timed compliments are more impactful than too many. Choose one or two that fit naturally into the conversation to keep the moment light and sincere.

4. Focus on the Moment

    - Compliments are best when they relate to the moment. If your date is telling a funny story, that's a perfect time to say *"Мені подобається твоє почуття гумору"* (I love your sense of humor), as it ties directly to the conversation.

5. Be Respectful

    - Avoid overly personal or intense compliments, especially early on. Compliments that feel too forward may make your date uncomfortable. Keep it simple and respectful to make a positive impression.

EXPRESSING INTEREST AND MAKING PLANS

Expressing interest and making plans for a date can be a crucial part of building a connection, especially when learning to navigate these interactions in a new language. Whether you're asking someone out or responding to an invitation, having the right phrases at your fingertips can boost your confidence and make the moment feel natural. This section provides practical Ukrainian phrases for asking someone out, discussing shared interests, and gracefully accepting or declining invitations, helping you communicate your intentions smoothly and respectfully.

Phrases for Asking Someone Out

When it comes to asking someone out, you want to sound friendly and genuine. Here are some essential phrases to express interest and invite someone to spend time with you:

- **Хотів/хотіла б ти якось зустрітися?** – Would you like to go out sometime?
  (*Example: Ти мені подобаєшся. Хотів/хотіла б ти якось зустрітися? – I like you. Would you like to go out sometime?*)

- **Може, вип'ємо щось?** – Shall we get a drink?
  (*Example: Може, вип'ємо щось після роботи? – Shall we get a drink after work?*)

- **Хотів/хотіла б ти піти зі мною в кіно?** – Would you like to go to the movies with me?
  (Example: Є фільм, який я хочу подивитися. Хотів/хотіла б ти піти зі мною в кіно? – There's a movie I want to see. Would you like to go to the movies with me?)

- **У тебе є плани на ці вихідні?** – Do you have plans for this weekend?
  (Example: У тебе є плани на ці вихідні? Я б із задоволенням провів/провела час із тобою. – Do you have plans for this weekend? I'd love to spend time with you.)

These phrases keep the tone light and open, allowing the other person to respond comfortably. When asking someone out, a warm smile and friendly body language can go a long way in showing genuine interest.

Discussing Shared Interests

Another great way to make plans is by suggesting an activity based on shared interests. This approach can feel more natural and emphasizes your mutual connection. Here are some phrases for expressing interest in doing something together:

- **Я б із задоволенням подивився/подивилася цей фільм з тобою** – I'd love to see that movie with you
  (Example: Я чув/чула, що тобі теж подобається цей фільм. Я б із задоволенням подивився/подивилася його з тобою. – I heard you like that movie too. I'd love to see it with you.)

- **Ми могли б піти в той ресторан, який тобі подобається** – We could go to that restaurant you like
  (*Example: Я знаю, що тобі подобається італійська кухня. Ми могли б піти в той ресторан, який тобі подобається. – I know you like Italian food. We could go to that restaurant you like.*)

- **Тобі подобається жива музика? У п'ятницю буде концерт** – Do you like live music? There's a concert this Friday
  (*Example: Тобі подобається жива музика? У п'ятницю буде концерт. Хотів/хотіла б піти? – Do you like live music? There's a concert this Friday. Would you like to go?*)

These types of invitations highlight your attentiveness to the other person's interests and can make the invitation feel more personal and engaging.

Accepting Invitations Politely

If someone invites you out, it's always nice to have polite ways to show your enthusiasm. Here are some ways to respond positively when someone asks you out:

- **Звичайно! Я б із задоволенням** – Of course! I'd love to
  (*Example: Звичайно! Я б із задоволенням пішов/пішла з тобою на вечерю. – Of course! I'd love to go to dinner with you.*)

- **Звучить чудово** – Sounds perfect
  (*Example: Може, вип'ємо кави в суботу? – Звучить чудово. – Shall we get coffee on Saturday? – Sounds perfect.*)

- **Дякую за запрошення, я б із задоволенням** – Thank you for inviting me, I'd love to
  (*Example:* Дякую за запрошення подивитися цей фільм. Я б із задоволенням пішов/пішла з тобою. – *Thank you for inviting me to see that movie. I'd love to go with you.*)

Accepting an invitation warmly lets the other person know that you're genuinely interested in spending time together and that you appreciate their invitation.

Politely Declining Invitations

Sometimes you may need to decline an invitation, but it's always best to do so politely. Here are some phrases that allow you to decline without being hurtful:

- **Дякую, але у мене є інші плани** – Thank you, but I have other plans
  (*Example:* Дякую за запрошення, але на той день у мене є інші плани. – *Thank you for inviting me, but I have other plans for that day.*)

- **Я б із задоволенням, але цього разу не можу** – I'd love to, but I can't this time
  (*Example:* Я б із задоволенням пішов/пішла з тобою на вечерю, але цього разу не можу. – *I'd love to go to dinner with you, but I can't this time.*)

- **Вибач, але, здається, я зайнятий/зайнята – I'm sorry, but I don't think I'm available**
  (Example: Вибач, але, здається, я зайнятий/зайнята на ці вихідні. – I'm sorry, but I don't think I'm available this weekend.)

These polite refusals allow you to set boundaries without causing discomfort. If appropriate, you can suggest another time to meet, which shows you're still interested in connecting despite the initial refusal.

CONVERSATION STARTERS AND KEEPING THE CONVERSATION GOING

Engaging someone in conversation is one of the best ways to create a genuine connection. In dating, conversation starters are especially important as they set the tone, reveal shared interests, and help you get to know each other on a deeper level. In this section, we'll explore meaningful questions that invite your date to share more about themselves, as well as lighter, playful questions to keep the mood fun and relaxed. By practicing these conversation starters and learning how to ask follow-up questions, you'll be able to navigate conversations confidently and keep things flowing naturally.

Meaningful Conversation Starters

Meaningful questions can open up deeper topics and allow your date to share personal stories or interests. Here are a few questions to help you connect on a more emotional level:

- **Яке твоє улюблене спогад із дитинства? – What's your favorite childhood memory?**
  (Example: Я люблю слухати історії з дитинства. Яке твоє улюблене спогад? – I love hearing childhood stories. What's your favorite childhood memory?)

- **Що тебе захоплює? – What are you passionate about?**
  (Example: Завжди цікаво дізнаватися про чиїсь захоплення. Що тебе захоплює? – It's always interesting to hear about someone's passions. What are you passionate about?)

- **Чого ти завжди хотів/хотіла навчитися? – What's something you've always wanted to learn?**
  (Example: Мені подобається ідея вчитися новому. Чого ти завжди хотів/хотіла навчитися? – I love the idea of learning new things. What's something you've always wanted to learn?)

- **Якби ти міг/могла подорожувати куди завгодно, куди б ти поїхав/поїхала? – If you could travel anywhere in the world, where would you go?**
  (Example: Ідея досліджувати світ — це чудово. Якби ти міг/могла подорожувати куди завгодно, куди б ти поїхав/поїхала? – The idea of exploring the world is amazing. If you could travel anywhere in the world, where would you go?)

These questions help create a comfortable space for your date to open up and share meaningful aspects of their life, creating a more memorable conversation.

Lighthearted Conversation Starters

In addition to meaningful topics, lighthearted questions keep the conversation fun and relaxed, helping to reduce any nervousness and encouraging a more playful tone. Here are some casual questions that can make the conversation feel more easy-going:

- **Тобі більше подобається пляж чи гори?** – Do you prefer the beach or the mountains?
  (Example: Це звичне питання, але завжди цікаве. Тобі більше подобається пляж чи гори? – It's a common question, but always interesting. Do you prefer the beach or the mountains?)

- **Яка твоя улюблена їжа?** – What's your favorite food?
  (Example: Я люблю пробувати нові страви. Яка твоя улюблена їжа? – I love trying new dishes. What's your favorite food?)

- **Якби ти був/була супергероєм, яку силу ти б мав/мала?** – If you were a superhero, what power would you have?
  (Example: Завжди весело уявляти. Якби ти був/була супергероєм, яку силу ти б мав/мала? – It's always fun to imagine. If you were a superhero, what power would you have?)

- **Як ти любиш проводити вихідні?** – What's your favorite way to spend the weekend?
  (Example: Завжди цікаво дізнаватися, як інші люблять відпочивати. Як ти любиш проводити вихідні? – It's interesting to know how others like to relax. What's your favorite way to spend the weekend?)

These questions add lightness to the conversation and encourage your date to share more about their personality in a relaxed way.

Tips for Keeping the Conversation Going

Once the conversation has started, keeping it flowing smoothly requires active listening and thoughtful responses. Here are a few tips to keep in mind:

1. **Ask Follow-Up Questions**

    - Showing genuine interest in their answers by asking follow-up questions makes the conversation feel natural and engaging. For example, if your date mentions a love for travel, you could ask, *"Яке місце здивувало тебе найбільше?"* (Which place surprised you the most?).

2. **Share Personal Stories**

    - Don't be afraid to share your own experiences or opinions in response to their answers. This creates a balanced conversation where both people feel heard and engaged.

3. **Pay Attention to Body Language**

    - Notice your date's body language to gauge their comfort level with certain topics. If they seem enthusiastic, continue exploring that topic. If they seem less interested, consider shifting the conversation to something new.

4. **Use Humor When Appropriate**

    - Light humor can keep things comfortable and fun. A playful response to their answer can ease any tension and make the interaction more enjoyable.

5. **Know When to Switch Topics**

    - If the conversation feels like it's slowing down, gently transition to a new question to keep the momentum going. This keeps the conversation fresh and prevents awkward pauses.

PHRASES FOR SHOWING AFFECTION AND BUILDING A CONNECTION

Expressing affection is a powerful way to strengthen a connection and show someone you care. In Ukrainian, affectionate phrases can range from simple expressions of appreciation to deeper statements that communicate emotional closeness. This section will introduce phrases for showing affection and building a connection, as well as tips on using affectionate language in a way that feels natural and appropriate. By learning these phrases, you'll be able to express your feelings in a warm and genuine way, whether on a date or through text.

Phrases for Showing Affection

Here are some phrases to help you show appreciation and affection. They are versatile and can be used in a variety of situations to make your partner feel valued and cared for.

- **Ти робиш мене щасливим/щасливою** – You make me happy
  (*Example: Кожного разу, коли ми разом, ти робиш мене щасливим/щасливою. – Every time we're together, you make me happy.*)

- **Мені дуже комфортно з тобою** – I feel very comfortable with you
  (*Example: З першого дня мені було дуже комфортно з тобою. – From the first day, I've felt very comfortable with you.*)

- **Ти важливий/важлива для мене** – You're important to me
  (Example: Я хочу, щоб ти знав/знала, що ти важливий/важлива для мене. – I want you to know that you're important to me.)

- **Я люблю проводити час із тобою** – I love spending time with you
  (Example: Мені завжди подобаються наші зустрічі. Я люблю проводити час із тобою. – I always enjoy our outings. I love spending time with you.)

- **Кожна мить із тобою особлива** – Every moment with you is special
  (Example: Неважливо, що ми робимо; кожна мить із тобою особлива. – It doesn't matter what we do; every moment with you is special.)

These phrases are gentle but heartfelt, making them suitable for both early stages of dating and more established relationships.

Building a Connection with Vulnerability

When building a connection, expressing vulnerability can deepen the relationship and create a sense of trust. Here are some phrases that allow you to share your feelings in a way that shows openness:

- **Я відчуваю, що можу бути собою з тобою** – I feel like I can be myself with you
  (Example: Це рідко трапляється, але я відчуваю, що можу бути собою з тобою. – It's rare, but I feel like I can be myself with you.)

- **Ти змушуєш мене відчувати себе особливим/особливою – You make me feel special**
  (Example: Кожного разу, коли ми розмовляємо, ти змушуєш мене відчувати себе особливим/особливою.– Every time we talk, you make me feel special.)

- **Я довіряю тобі – I trust you**
  (Example: З тобою легко говорити; я довіряю тобі. – It's easy to talk to you; I trust you.)

Vulnerability can be a powerful way to connect, but it's essential to approach it thoughtfully, especially early on. Using phrases like these sparingly and at the right moments can make them feel more meaningful.

Tips for Using Affectionate Language Naturally

When expressing affection, consider these tips to ensure your words feel genuine and comfortable:

1. **Start with Light Compliments**

    - In the early stages of a relationship, keep your affectionate language light and relaxed. Phrases like *"Я люблю проводити час із тобою"* (I love spending time with you) are ideal for showing interest without being too intense.

2. **Be Mindful of Timing**

    - Context matters when expressing affection. If you're on a first date, keep your expressions of affection simple and sincere. As the relationship deepens, you can gradually use phrases that communicate stronger feelings.

3. **Match Your Words with Actions**

    - Actions often speak louder than words. A sincere smile, maintaining eye contact, or giving small gestures of kindness can make your words feel even more genuine.

4. **Observe the Other Person's Reactions**

    - Pay attention to your partner's responses. If they seem comfortable, continue expressing affection. If they seem hesitant, ease back and focus on building trust through shared experiences.

5. **Keep it Authentic**

    - Speak from the heart and avoid overly dramatic expressions. Simple phrases, spoken sincerely, often feel more genuine and impactful.

DEALING WITH MISUNDERSTANDINGS AND AWKWARD MOMENTS

Misunderstandings are a natural part of any relationship, especially when communicating in a different language or culture. Learning how to handle these moments gracefully can help you navigate dating interactions with confidence and show respect for your partner's perspective. In this section, you'll learn useful phrases in Ukrainian to clarify confusion and reassure your partner, along with tips for managing awkward pauses and handling missed cultural cues. By practicing these strategies, you'll be prepared to address misunderstandings calmly and maintain a positive atmosphere in your interactions.

Phrases to Clarify Confusion Politely

If you didn't catch something your date said or need them to clarify, using polite language can make the request feel more comfortable. Here are some phrases to help you ask for clarification in a respectful way:

- **Здається, я тебе неправильно зрозумів/зрозуміла – I think I didn't understand you well**
  (Example: Вибач, здається, я тебе неправильно зрозумів/зрозуміла. Можеш повторити? – Sorry, I think I didn't understand you well. Could you repeat that?)

- **Можеш сказати це інакше? – Could you say it in another way?**
  (Example: Можеш сказати це інакше? Я не впевнений/впевнена, що зрозумів/зрозуміла. – Could you say it in another way? I'm not sure I understand.)

- **Можеш пояснити трохи детальніше? – Could you explain it a bit more?**
  (Example: Можеш пояснити трохи детальніше? Я хочу бути впевненим/впевненою, що правильно тебе розумію. – Could you explain it a bit more? I want to make sure I understand you well.)

- **Ти маєш на увазі...? – Are you referring to…?**
  (Example: Ти маєш на увазі те, що казав/казала раніше? Я хочу переконатися. – Are you referring to what you mentioned before? I want to be sure.)

These phrases show a willingness to understand and can be especially helpful when navigating new expressions or slang you may not be familiar with.

Reassuring Phrases for Diffusing Tension

If a misunderstanding occurs or an awkward moment arises, reassuring your date can ease any discomfort and keep the conversation light. Here are some phrases to help diffuse tension or reassure your partner if they feel they've made a mistake:

- **Не переймайся, ми всі робимо помилки – Don't worry, we all make mistakes**
  (Example: Не переймайся, ми всі робимо помилки. Це частина навчання. – Don't worry, we all make mistakes. It's part of learning.)

- **Це нормально, таке трапляється з усіма – It's normal, it happens to everyone**
  (Example: Це нормально, таке трапляється з усіма. Іноді важко висловити свої думки. – It's normal, it happens to everyone. Sometimes it's hard to express oneself.)

- **Нічого страшного – It's okay / It's no big deal**
  (Example: Все добре, головне, що ти спробував/спробувала. – It's okay, the important thing is that you tried.)

- **Я розумію; легко заплутатися – I understand; it's easy to get confused**
  (Example: Я розумію; легко заплутатися, коли говоримо про складні речі. – I understand; it's easy to get confused when we talk about complex things.)

Reassuring phrases like these show empathy and understanding, which can help make your partner feel more comfortable, especially if they're also navigating language differences.

Tips for Handling Awkward Pauses and Missed Cultural Cues

Misunderstandings aren't always verbal; sometimes, they come from differences in body language, humor, or cultural cues. Here are some tips to help you handle these moments gracefully:

1. **Use Humor to Ease Tension**

    - Light humor can help relieve awkwardness. If there's a long pause or you realize you missed a cue, a friendly smile or a lighthearted comment like *"Ой, здається, я щось пропустив/пропустила"* (Oops, it seems like I missed something) can help break the tension.

2. **Acknowledge the Moment**

    - If you sense a cultural misunderstanding, acknowledge it gently. For example, *"Я не впевнений/впевнена, чи правильно зрозумів/зрозуміла, але хочу дізнатися більше"* (I'm not sure if I understood correctly, but I'd like to learn) can show openness to understanding their perspective.

3. **Stay Patient and Listen**

    - Give your partner time to explain or clarify without rushing them. Patience demonstrates respect and gives the other person space to express themselves in their own words.

4. **Be Aware of Body Language**

    - Watch for non-verbal cues like nodding, eye contact, or crossed arms, which can give you clues about how the other person is feeling. If they seem uncomfortable, ease into a new topic or ask an open question to redirect the conversation.

5. **Ask Open-Ended Questions**

    - If there's an awkward pause, asking an open-ended question, such as *"Що ти думаєш про...?"* (What do you think about...?) can help keep the conversation flowing. Open questions allow your partner to respond in more detail, which can bring new energy to the interaction.

By keeping these tips in mind, you'll be better prepared to handle any uncomfortable moments or cultural differences that might arise in a relaxed and respectful way.

NAVIGATING BOUNDARIES AND RELATIONSHIP EXPECTATIONS

Navigating boundaries is essential for building a healthy and respectful connection in any relationship. In dating, setting clear boundaries and understanding each other's expectations can help prevent misunderstandings and create a foundation of trust. This section provides useful phrases in Ukrainian for expressing boundaries and discussing relationship expectations. By learning these phrases, you'll feel more confident in expressing your needs and understanding your partner's perspective.

Phrases for Expressing Boundaries

Clear communication about boundaries helps ensure that both people in a relationship feel comfortable and respected. Here are some phrases in Ukrainian to help you express your boundaries in a way that encourages open dialogue and understanding:

- **Мені було б комфортніше, якби... – I would feel more comfortable if...**
  (Example: Мені було б комфортніше, якби ми не поспішали. – I would feel more comfortable if we took things slowly.)

- **Я б віддав/віддала перевагу, щоб... – I'd prefer that...**
  (Example: Я б віддав/віддала перевагу, щоб ми поговорили про наші очікування. – I'd prefer that we talk about our expectations.)

- **Для мене важливо, щоб...** – For me, it's important that...
  (Example: Для мене важливо, щоб ми поважали одне одного. – For me, it's important that we respect each other.)

- **Мені некомфортно з...** – I don't feel comfortable with...
  (Example: Мені некомфортно поспішати. – I don't feel comfortable rushing things.)

Using these phrases helps you communicate your needs in a way that's both clear and respectful, encouraging your partner to understand and respect your boundaries.

Phrases for Discussing Relationship Expectations

When dating, it's natural to want to understand each other's intentions and expectations. Here are some phrases to help you discuss relationship goals, which can guide you toward a deeper connection or clarify if you're both on the same page:

- **Що ти шукаєш у стосунках?** – What are you looking for in a relationship?
  (Example: Щоб краще розуміти одне одного, що ти шукаєш у стосунках? – To understand each other better, what are you looking for in a relationship?)

- **Ти хочеш чогось серйозного чи чогось більш легкого?** – Would you like something serious or something casual?
  (Example: Хочу бути чесним/чесною: ти хочеш чогось серйозного чи чогось більш легкого? – I want to be honest, would you like something serious or something casual?)

- **Які твої очікування від цих стосунків?** – What are your expectations in this relationship?
  (Example: Важливо знати: які твої очікування від цих стосунків? – It's important to know: what are your expectations in this relationship?)

- **Для мене важливо бути чесним/чесною щодо того, чого я хочу** – For me, it's important to be honest about what I want
  (Example: Для мене важливо бути чесним/чесною щодо того, чого я хочу, і мені цікаво дізнатися твою думку. – For me, it's important to be honest about what I want, and I'd like to know your thoughts too.)

These phrases open the door for a transparent discussion, helping both people feel understood and supported in their expectations.

Tips for Discussing Feelings and Boundaries Respectfully

When discussing boundaries and expectations, maintaining respect and openness is key to keeping the conversation positive. Here are some tips to help you communicate with empathy:

1. **Choose the Right Time**

    - Pick a calm, relaxed moment for these conversations to ensure both of you are attentive and comfortable. Avoid bringing up boundaries or expectations during moments of tension or when either of you feels rushed.

2. **Use "I" Statements**

    - Phrasing things from your own perspective can reduce defensiveness and make the conversation feel more constructive. For instance, saying *"Я віддаю перевагу не поспішати"* (I prefer to take things slowly) feels less imposing than *"Треба робити все поступово"* (You have to take things slowly).

3. **Listen Actively**

    - Give your partner the chance to express their thoughts without interrupting, and show you're listening with responses like *"Я розумію"* (I understand) or *"Дякую, що поділився/поділилася цим зі мною"* (thank you for sharing that with me).

4. Stay Open and Non-Judgmental

    - Everyone has unique perspectives and experiences. If your partner's boundaries or expectations differ from yours, respond with understanding, such as *"Я вдячний/вдячна, що ти мені це сказав/сказала"* (I appreciate you telling me) or *"Дякую за твою щирість"* (Thank you for being honest).

5. Reassure Each Other

    - Let your partner know that discussing boundaries and expectations is a positive step. Reassuring phrases like *"Добре знати, чого хоче кожен із нас"* (It's good to know what each of us wants) or *"Ми можемо не поспішати"* (We can take our time) can help both of you feel more secure in the relationship.

By keeping these tips in mind, you can handle these important conversations smoothly and respectfully, building a foundation of trust and openness.

SAYING GOODBYE: PHRASES FOR ENDING DATES OR CONVERSATIONS GRACEFULLY

The way you say goodbye after a date can leave a lasting impression. Whether it's a friendly closing, an enthusiastic hint about seeing each other again, or a polite way to decline future dates, your parting words can communicate interest, respect, and sincerity. In this section, we'll explore different ways to say goodbye in Ukrainian, including casual phrases for friendly farewells, expressions of interest in future dates, and polite ways to decline additional meetups if you don't see the connection progressing.

Casual Closings for Friendly Farewells

Sometimes, a simple, friendly farewell is all you need to close the date on a positive note. Here are some casual closings that work well if you've enjoyed your time but want to keep it light:

- **Побачимося пізніше** – See you later
  (Example: Дякую за сьогоднішній вечір, побачимося пізніше! – Thanks for tonight, see you later!)

- **До скорої зустрічі** – See you soon
  (Example: Мені дуже сподобалося. До скорої зустрічі. – I had a great time. See you soon.)

- **Бережи себе** – Take care
  (Example: Бережи себе, було приємно познайомитися. – Take care; it was nice meeting you.)

- **Гарної ночі** – Have a good night
  (Example: Було приємно провести час із тобою. Гарної ночі. – It was a pleasure going out with you. Have a good night.)

These closings are warm and casual, making them ideal for dates where you feel comfortable but aren't quite ready to express strong intentions for the future.

Expressing Interest in Future Dates

If you want to see your date again, use phrases that show interest without being too forward. Here are some examples:

- **Я б із задоволенням зустрівся/зустрілася з тобою знову** – I'd love to see you again
  (Example: Сьогодні ввечері мені було дуже приємно. Я б із задоволенням зустрівся/зустрілася з тобою знову. – I had a great time tonight. I'd love to see you again.)

- **Сподіваюся, ми зможемо повторити це** – Hopefully, we can do this again
  (Example: Мені було дуже весело. Сподіваюся, ми зможемо повторити це. – I had a lot of fun. Hopefully, we can do this again.)

- **Дай знати, якщо ти хотів/хотіла б зустрітися знову** – Let me know if you'd like to go out again
  (Example: Це був веселий вечір. Дай знати, якщо ти хотів/хотіла б зустрітися знову. – It was a fun night. Let me know if you'd like to go out again.)

- **Я сподіваюся побачити тебе скоро** – I hope to see you soon
  (Example: Мені сподобалося проводити час із тобою. Я сподіваюся побачити тебе скоро. – I enjoyed spending time with you. I hope to see you soon.)

These phrases communicate interest and leave the door open for future dates, allowing your date to feel appreciated without any pressure.

Polite Ways to Decline Future Dates

Sometimes, you may not feel a connection strong enough to pursue another date. In these cases, it's important to be kind but clear. Here are polite ways to let your date know you're not interested in seeing them again while still showing respect:

- **Було приємно познайомитися, але, здається, ми дивимося на речі по-різному** – It was a pleasure meeting you, but I think we're not on the same page
  (Example: Було приємно познайомитися, але, здається, ми шукаємо різні речі. – It was a pleasure meeting you, but I think we're not on the same page regarding what we're looking for.)

- **Мені було добре, але, здається, ми шукаємо різні речі** – I had a good time, but I think we're looking for different things
  (Example: Дякую за компанію. Мені було добре, але, здається, ми шукаємо різні речі. – Thanks for the company. I had a good time, but I think we're looking for different things.)

- **Я вдячний/вдячна за вечір, але я не зацікавлений/зацікавлена у ще одній зустрічі** – I appreciate the evening, but I'm not interested in another date
  (Example: Я вдячний/вдячна за вечір, але я не зацікавлений/зацікавлена у ще одній зустрічі. – I appreciate the evening, but I'm not interested in another date.)

- **Ти чудова людина, але я не відчуваю романтичного зв'язку** – You're a great person, but I don't feel a romantic connection
  (Example: Ти чудова людина, але я не відчуваю романтичного зв'язку. Бажаю тобі всього найкращого. – You're a great person, but I don't feel a romantic connection. I wish you the best.)

Using these phrases allows you to express your feelings kindly and clearly, making the goodbye more comfortable for both you and your date.

DIGITAL FLIRTING: BUILDING CONNECTIONS THROUGH TEXT

In today's dating world, digital flirting—whether through texts, social media, or dating apps—has become an essential skill. Texting allows for a more relaxed and playful form of interaction, helping you express interest, get to know someone, and build anticipation for an in-person meeting. In this section, you'll learn key phrases in Ukrainian for starting and maintaining a conversation through text, as well as tips on transitioning smoothly from digital exchanges to planning a date.

Starting a Text Conversation

The first message sets the tone for the entire interaction. Whether you're following up after a date or starting a chat on a dating app, a warm and genuine greeting can make the conversation feel comfortable from the start. Here are some phrases in Ukrainian to help you kick things off:

- **Привіт, сподіваюся, у тебе все добре – Hi, I hope you're well**
  (Example: Привіт, сподіваюся, у тебе все добре. Я згадав/згадала нашу розмову і хотів/хотіла сказати привіт. – Hi, I hope you're well. I remembered our conversation and wanted to say hello.)

- **Як проходить твій день? – How's your day going?**
  (Example: Привіт! Як проходить твій день? – Hi! How's your day going?)

- **Мені дуже сподобалося знайомство з тобою вчора, як ти?** – I loved meeting you yesterday, how are you?
  (Example: Мені дуже сподобалося знайомство з тобою вчора, як ти? Хотів/хотіла б підтримувати зв'язок? – I loved meeting you yesterday, how are you? Would you like to stay in touch?)

- **Привіт! Я просто хотів/хотіла сказати, що це нагадало мені про тебе** – Hi! I just wanted to say that this made me think of you
  (Example: Привіт! Я подивився/подивилася фільм, про який ти згадував/згадувала, і це нагадало мені про тебе. – Hi! I saw a movie you mentioned, and it made me think of you.)

Starting with a friendly, thoughtful message shows interest without pressure and helps build rapport, encouraging the conversation to flow naturally.

Keeping the Conversation Going

Once the conversation has started, keeping it engaging is key to building a connection. Open-ended questions are especially effective, as they invite more detailed responses, allowing you to get to know each other better. Here are some examples of questions that can keep the conversation flowing:

- **Яка найкраща річ трапилася з тобою цього тижня?** – What's the best thing that happened to you this week?
  (Example: Яка найкраща річ трапилася з тобою цього тижня? Мені хотілося б більше дізнатися про тебе. – What's the best thing that happened to you this week? I'd love to know more about you.)

- **Якби ти міг/могла подорожувати куди завгодно прямо зараз, куди б ти поїхав/поїхала? – If you could travel anywhere right now, where would you go?**
  (*Example: Якби ти міг/могла подорожувати куди завгодно прямо зараз, куди б ти поїхав/поїхала? Мені було б цікаво почути про твої мрії-подорожі. – If you could travel anywhere right now, where would you go? I'd love to hear about your dream adventures.*)

- **У тебе є улюблені фільми чи серіали, які ти міг/могла б порекомендувати? – Do you have any favorite movies or shows you'd recommend?**
  (*Example: У тебе є улюблені фільми чи серіали, які ти міг/могла б порекомендувати? Я завжди шукаю щось нове для перегляду. – Do you have any favorite movies or shows you'd recommend? I'm always looking for something new to watch.*)

- **Що тебе захоплює? – What's something you're passionate about?**
  (*Example: Що тебе захоплює? Мені хотілося б більше дізнатися про твої інтереси. – What's something you're passionate about? I'd like to know more about your interests.*)

Using open-ended questions helps keep the conversation engaging and allows you to show genuine curiosity about the other person. Remember to actively listen to their responses and respond with comments that build on what they share.

Transitioning from Texting to Planning an In-Person Date

If the conversation is going well and you sense that the interest is mutual, you might want to suggest meeting in person. Here are some phrases to smoothly transition from texting to planning a date:

- **Хотів/хотіла б ти якось зустрітися? –** Would you like to go out sometime?
  (Example: Мені подобається спілкуватися з тобою, хотів/хотіла б ти якось зустрітися? – I enjoy talking to you, would you like to go out sometime?)

- **Як щодо того, щоб випити кави або прогулятися? –** How about grabbing a coffee or going for a walk?
  (Example: Як щодо того, щоб випити кави або прогулятися? Було б приємно поспілкуватися особисто. – How about grabbing a coffee or going for a walk? It'd be nice to chat in person.)

- **Я хотів/хотіла б зустрітися з тобою особисто, як щодо цих вихідних? –** I'd like to see you in person, how about this weekend?
  (Example: Я хотів/хотіла б зустрітися з тобою особисто, як щодо цих вихідних? Думаю, це було б весело. – I'd like to see you in person, how about this weekend? I think it'd be fun.)

- **Дай знати, якщо ти хотів/хотіла б щось зробити разом – Let me know if you'd like to do something together**
  (Example: Дай знати, якщо ти хотів/хотіла б щось зробити разом. Я б із задоволенням провів/провела більше часу з тобою. – Let me know if you'd like to do something together. I'd love to spend more time with you.)

These phrases express your interest in a gentle and open way, giving your date the chance to accept or suggest an alternative. This keeps the conversation relaxed while showing you're genuinely interested in spending time together.

Tips for Digital Flirting

When flirting through text, here are a few tips to keep the exchange natural, friendly, and engaging:

1. **Keep Your Messages Light and Friendly**

   - Start with simple, lighthearted messages to build comfort. Texting is typically more casual than in-person conversation, so feel free to keep the tone friendly and relaxed.

2. **Avoid Over-Texting**

   - Give each other space to respond. Texting too frequently can sometimes feel overwhelming. Aim for a balanced pace where both people have a chance to contribute to the conversation.

3. **Use Emojis to Add Personality**

   - Emojis can help convey emotion and make your messages feel more personable. Use them sparingly to add warmth or humor without overdoing it.

4. **Show Genuine Interest**

   - Respond thoughtfully to what the other person shares, rather than focusing solely on yourself. This shows you're interested in getting to know them.

5. **Be Confident but Respectful When Suggesting a Date**

   - When you're ready to transition to an in-person date, suggest it confidently but leave space for their response. If they agree, great! If they seem unsure, you can keep chatting and wait for the right time.

ENDING RELATIONSHIPS POLITELY: NAVIGATING BREAKUPS WITH RESPECT

While ending a relationship is never easy, doing so with respect and empathy can make a difficult conversation more bearable for both people involved. In Ukrainian, there are gentle and compassionate ways to communicate that you're ready to part ways, allowing both parties to move on gracefully. This section will provide phrases to help you end relationships politely, along with tips for managing these conversations with empathy and kindness.

Phrases for Ending Relationships Respectfully

Choosing the right words when ending a relationship is important for preserving respect and understanding. Here are some Ukrainian phrases to help you communicate your decision in a way that is honest yet gentle:

- **Думаю, нам краще розійтися** – I think it's best we go our separate ways
  (Example: Після роздумів я думаю, що нам краще розійтися. – After thinking it over, I think it's best we go our separate ways.)

- **Я не хочу тебе образити, але думаю, настав час рухатися далі** – I don't want to hurt you, but I think it's time to move on
  (*Example: Я не хочу тебе образити, але думаю, настав час рухатися далі. Сподіваюся, ти розумієш. – I don't want to hurt you, but I think it's time to move on. I hope you understand.*)

- **Я відчуваю, що ми обоє заслуговуємо на щось інше** – I feel that we both deserve something different
  (*Example: Я відчуваю, що ми обоє заслуговуємо на щось інше, і нам буде краще так. – I feel that we both deserve something different and that we'll be happier this way.*)

- **Так буде краще для нас обох, якщо ми завершимо це тут** – It's better for both of us if we end things here
  (*Example: Я дійшов/дійшла висновку, що так буде краще для нас обох, якщо ми завершимо це тут. Кажу це з усією повагою. – I've come to the conclusion that it's better for both of us if we end things here. I say this with all respect.*)

These phrases allow you to be direct while expressing a desire for a positive outcome for both people, helping to ease any potential hurt.

Reassuring Phrases to Show Kindness and Understanding

In addition to ending the relationship, expressing well-wishes or appreciation can leave a positive final impression. Here are some reassuring phrases to use when closing the conversation:

- **Я сподіваюся, ти знайдеш когось, хто зробить тебе щасливим/щасливою** – I hope you find someone who makes you happy
  (Example: Ти чудова людина, і я сподіваюся, ти знайдеш когось, хто зробить тебе щасливим/щасливою. – You're a good person, and I hope you find someone who makes you happy.)

- **Дякую за ті моменти, які ми провели разом** – Thank you for the moments we shared
  (Example: Дякую за ті моменти, які ми провели разом; я завжди буду згадувати їх із теплотою. – Thank you for the moments we shared; I'll always remember them fondly.)

- **Бажаю тобі всього найкращого в майбутньому** – I wish you the best in the future
  (Example: Бажаю тобі всього найкращого в майбутньому і сподіваюся, що ти знайдеш багато щастя. – I wish you the best in the future, and I hope you find much happiness.)

- **Ти особлива людина, і я завжди буду мати гарні спогади про тебе** – You're a special person, and I'll always have good memories of you
  (Example: Ти особлива людина, і я завжди буду мати гарні спогади про тебе, навіть після цього. – You're a special person, and I'll always have good memories of you, even after this.)

These phrases add warmth to the conversation and can help the other person feel appreciated, even as you part ways. Small gestures of kindness can soften the impact and show that you truly wish them well.

Tips for Ending Relationships with Empathy

Managing a breakup with empathy can make the experience more positive for both people involved. Here are some tips to help guide your approach:

1. Choose a Private, Comfortable Setting

    - Select a place where both of you can talk openly without distractions. A quiet, neutral space allows for privacy and makes it easier to have an honest conversation.

2. Be Honest but Gentle

    - Be direct, but avoid harsh language or criticism. Statements like *"Ти не та людина, яка мені підходить"* (you're not the right person for me) are more constructive than saying what you don't like about them.

3. Listen and Acknowledge Their Feelings

   - Give the other person a chance to express themselves, and listen to their perspective. You can show you're listening by responding with phrases like *"Я розумію, як ти почуваєшся"* (I understand how you feel).

4. Avoid Giving False Hope

   - Be clear in your intentions so they don't hold onto false hope. Gentle but firm language like *"Так буде краще для нас обох, якщо ми підемо далі"* (it's better for both of us if we move on) reinforces your decision kindly.

5. Express Appreciation for the Relationship

   - Acknowledging the good moments can help both of you part on better terms. Thanking them for the experiences you shared makes it clear that you value the time spent together, even if it's time to move forward separately.

6. Give Space After the Conversation

   - Offer a bit of space following the conversation, allowing both of you to process the emotions involved. A respectful, simple goodbye is often the best way to end the conversation.

Handling these conversations with respect and understanding can help you close this chapter on a positive note, allowing both of you to move on in a healthy way.

CHAPTER FIVE:
CONVERSATIONS & DIALOGUES FOR DIFFERENT SCENARIOS

MEETING SOMEONE FOR THE FIRST TIME

Meeting someone for the first time can feel a bit intimidating, especially if you're navigating language and cultural differences. In this section, we'll cover the essentials for creating a positive first impression in Ukrainian. You'll learn common greetings, introductions, and conversation starters, all designed to help you feel confident and approachable when meeting someone new in a romantic setting.

Greetings and Introductions

The greeting is your first chance to make a good impression. In Ukrainian, greetings can vary depending on the time of day and level of formality, but here are some versatile options:

- **Привіт, як справи?**
  (Hi, how are you?)

- **Добрий вечір, приємно познайомитися**
  (Good evening, a pleasure to meet you)

- **Приємно познайомитися, я [ваше ім'я]**
  (Nice to meet you, I'm [your name])

For a first-time meeting in a relaxed or social setting, using *"Привіт"* or *"Приємно познайомитися"* feels friendly without being too formal. Remember to follow up your greeting with a simple smile and eye contact, which can make a big difference in building a connection.

Basic Questions to Start the Conversation

After your initial greeting, opening with light questions shows interest and keeps the conversation moving naturally. Here are a few go-to questions that help get to know someone without being intrusive:

- **Звідки ви? – Where are you from?**
  (*Example response:* Я з Лос-Анджелеса, але живу тут вже кілька років. – *I'm from Los Angeles, but I've lived here for a few years.*)

- **Що привело вас сюди? – What brings you here?**
  (*Example response:* Я приїхав/приїхала на захід; мені подобається знайомитися з новими людьми. – *I came for the event; I love meeting new people.*)

- **Чим ви займаєтеся? – What do you do?**
  (*Example response:* Я графічний дизайнер. – *I'm a graphic designer.*)

- **Вам подобається це місце? – Do you like this place?**
  (*Example response:* Так, воно дуже затишне. – *Yes, it's very cozy.*)

These questions are ideal for a casual setting, such as meeting someone at a café or social event, where people are often open to conversation.

Sample Dialogue: A First Encounter at a Café

To illustrate how these greetings and questions flow in a conversation, here's a sample dialogue. Imagine two people, Cameron and Sally, meeting for the first time at a coffee shop event.

Cameron: Привіт, як справи?
(Hi, how are you?)

Sally: Привіт, дуже добре, дякую. А у вас?
(Hi, very well, thanks. And you?)

Cameron: Добре, дякую. Приємно познайомитися, я Кемерон.
(Good, thanks. Nice to meet you; I'm Cameron.)

Sally: Приємно познайомитися, Кемерон. Я Саллі.
(Nice to meet you, Cameron. I'm Sally.)

Cameron: Звідки ви, Саллі?
(Where are you from, Sally?)

Sally: Я з Австралії, але я тут у гостях. А ви?
(I'm from Australia, but I'm visiting here. And you?)

Cameron: Я звідси. Що привело вас сюди?
(I'm from here. What brings you here?)

Sally: Я приїхав/приїхала на мистецький захід і хотів/хотіла трохи дослідити місто.
(I came for an art event, and I wanted to explore the city a bit.)

Cameron: Це чудово, тут багато цікавих місць. Вам подобається це кафе?
(That's great, there are a lot of interesting places here. Do you like this café?)

Sally: Так, воно дуже затишне, а кава смачна.
(Yes, it's very cozy, and the coffee is delicious.)

Cameron: Повністю згоден/згодна. Хотіли б, щоб я порекомендував/порекомендувала ще якісь місця?
(Totally agree. Would you like me to recommend other places?)

In this dialogue, Cameron and Sally's conversation flows naturally from greetings to asking about each other's background and plans. Cameron shows interest in Sally's experience in the city, while Sally responds with warmth and friendliness, which keeps the interaction engaging.

SMALL TALK: KEEPING IT LIGHT AND FUN

Small talk is an essential skill in any language, especially in social and dating contexts. When you're getting to know someone, keeping the conversation light and fun can help build a comfortable atmosphere. In this section, we'll go over useful phrases and topics for casual conversation in Ukrainian, focusing on approachable, friendly questions that don't go too deep too soon.

Topics and Phrases for Casual Conversation

Small talk in Ukrainian is similar to small talk in English, often covering topics like preferences, hobbies, or general interests. Here are some common questions and topics that can help break the ice:

1. **Personal Preferences**

   These questions are simple but can reveal shared interests and spark further conversation.

   - **Ви надаєте перевагу пляжу чи горам?** – Do you prefer the beach or the mountains?
     (*Example answer: Я віддаю перевагу горам; я люблю походи.* – *I prefer the mountains; I love hiking.*)

   - **Яка ваша улюблена пора року?** – What's your favorite season of the year?
     (*Example answer: Я люблю літо, бо можу більше часу проводити на свіжому повітрі.* – *I love summer because I can spend more time outdoors.*)

2. Movies, Music, and Books

Talking about entertainment is a great way to find common ground.

- **У вас є улюблений фільм? – Do you have a favorite movie?**
  (Example answer: Так, я люблю «Амелі». Я дивився/дивилася його багато разів. – Yes, I love 'Amélie'. I've seen it many times.)

- **Яку музику ви любите? – What type of music do you like?**
  (Example answer: Я слухаю все, але рок — мій улюблений жанр. – I listen to everything, but rock is my favorite.)

3. Food and Dining

Food is a universally enjoyable topic, and talking about favorite dishes can make the conversation lively.

- **У вас є улюблений ресторан поблизу? – Do you have a favorite restaurant around here?**
  (Example answer: Так, мені дуже подобається «Бобс Бургерс». Їхня їжа смачна.– Yes, I really like 'Bob's Burgers'. Their food is delicious.)

- **Вам подобається готувати? – Do you like to cook?**
  (Example answer: Так, я люблю готувати, особливо італійські страви. – Yes, I enjoy cooking, especially Italian dishes.)

4. Hobbies and Free Time

Asking about someone's hobbies is a natural way to learn more about their personality.

- **Чим ви любите займатися у вільний час? – What do you like to do in your free time?**
  (Example answer: Мені подобається читати й гуляти. – I like reading and going for walks.)

- **Ви займаєтеся якимись видами спорту? – Do you play any sports?**
  (Example answer: Я граю в теніс на вихідних. – I play tennis on weekends.)

Each of these questions offers a quick way to get a conversation going, allowing the other person to share something about themselves while keeping the tone light and casual.

Example Dialogue: A Friendly Small-Talk Exchange

To show how these phrases work in a real conversation, here's a sample dialogue between Cameron and Lucy as they chat at a casual gathering.

Cameron: Привіт, Люсі. Все добре?
(Hi, Lucy. Everything good?)

Lucy: Привіт, Кемерон. Так, усе добре. А у вас?
(Hi, Cameron. Yes, all good. And you?)

Cameron: Усе добре, дякую. До речі, цікаво — ви надаєте перевагу пляжу чи горам?
(All good, thanks. Hey, I'm curious—do you prefer the beach or the mountains?)

Lucy: О, складний вибір. Думаю, я надаю перевагу горам; я люблю походи.
(Ooh, tough choice. I think I prefer the mountains; I love hiking.)

Cameron: Я теж. Нічого не зрівняється зі свіжим повітрям у горах. У вас є улюблений фільм?
(Me too. Nothing like the fresh air in the mountains. Do you have a favorite movie?)

Lucy: Так, мені дуже подобається «Амелі». Воно завжди змушує мене усміхатися.
(Yes, I really like 'Amélie'. It always makes me smile.)

Cameron: Гарний вибір. Це унікальний фільм. А скажіть, яку музику ви любите?
(Good choice. It's a unique film. And tell me, what type of music do you like?)

Lucy: Я слухаю все, але джаз мене дуже розслабляє. А ви?
(I listen to everything, but jazz really relaxes me. And you?)

Cameron: Я теж люблю джаз, особливо для роботи. Ви відвідували концерти останнім часом?
(I like jazz too, especially for working. Have you been to any concerts lately?)

Lucy: Ні, давно ні, але я б із задоволенням пішов/пішла. Вам доведеться щось порекомендувати!
(No, it's been a while, but I'd love to go. You'll have to recommend one to me!)

This dialogue shows how small talk can flow smoothly from one topic to another, moving from preferences to hobbies. Cameron and Lucy keep the conversation casual, light, and engaging, with each question naturally leading into the next.

MAKING PLANS TOGETHER

Inviting someone out is a natural step forward in any connection, whether it's a casual hangout or a romantic date. In Ukrainian, there are many ways to propose plans, from a simple coffee to a weekend outing. This section will introduce key phrases for making invitations and example dialogues for different types of dates.

Phrases for Inviting Someone Out

Inviting someone to spend time with you is often about choosing the right words and gauging their response. Here are some friendly phrases you can use:

- **Хотіли б якось зустрітися?** – Would you like to go out sometime?
  (Example: Я б із задоволенням дізнався/дізналася більше про вас. Хотіли б якось зустрітися? – I'd love to get to know you better. Would you like to go out sometime?)

- **Як щодо того, щоб випити щось цими вихідними?** – How about we go for a drink this weekend?
  (Example: Як щодо того, щоб випити щось цими вихідними? Я знаю гарне місце. – How about we go for a drink this weekend? I know a nice place.)

- **Хотіли б випити кави разом?** – Would you like to have coffee together?
  (Example: Я б із задоволенням запросив/запросила вас на каву. Хотіли б випити разом? – I'd love to invite you for coffee. Would you like to have one together?)

- **Хотіли б піти в кіно?** – Would you like to go to the movies?
  (Example: Скоро виходить фільм, який я хочу подивитися. Хотіли б піти в кіно? – A movie I want to see is coming out. Would you like to go to the movies?)

- **У вас є плани на цю суботу? Ми могли б зробити щось веселе.** – Do you have plans this Saturday? We could do something fun.
  (Example: У вас є плани на цю суботу? Ми могли б зробити щось веселе та трохи розслабитися. – Do you have plans this Saturday? We could do something fun and relax a bit.)

These phrases give the other person room to respond and create a friendly, open invitation. Make sure to express interest while allowing them to comfortably accept or decline based on their schedule and comfort level.

Example Dialogues for Different Types of Dates

Let's take a look at how these phrases work in conversations. On the following pages are example dialogues for inviting someone to different kinds of outings, such as a casual coffee or a weekend event.

Dialogue 1: Inviting Someone for Coffee

Imagine Daniel and Clara have been chatting and Daniel wants to invite Clara out for coffee.

Daniel: Мені дуже подобається спілкуватися з вами. Хотіли б випити кави разом?
(I love talking with you. Would you like to have coffee together?)

Clara: Звичайно, я б із задоволенням. У вас є ідея, де це зробити?
(Sure, I'd love to. Do you have a place in mind?)

Daniel: Так, я знаю затишне кафе неподалік. Як щодо завтра о п'ятій?
(Yes, I know a cozy café nearby. How about tomorrow at five?)

Clara: Ідеально, я буду там.
(Perfect, I'll be there.)

Dialogue 2: Suggesting a Movie Date

In this example, Laura and James are discussing their favorite movies, and James sees an opportunity to invite Laura to a new film.

James: Ви казали, що вам подобаються науково-фантастичні фільми, так?
(You told me you like sci-fi movies, right?)

Laura: Так, я їх люблю. Ви знаєте якийсь хороший?
(Yes, I love them. Do you know of a good one?)

James: Так, скоро виходить новий. Хотіли б піти в кіно цими вихідними?
(Yes, a new one is coming out. Would you like to go to the movies this weekend?)

Laura: Звичайно! Коли б вам було зручно піти?
(Of course! When would you like to go?)

James: Як щодо суботнього вечора? Я можу заїхати за вами о сьомій.
(How about Saturday evening? I can pick you up at seven.)

Laura: Чудово, звучить ідеально!
(Great, sounds perfect!)

Dialogue 3: Planning a Weekend Outing

This time, Sofia and Lucas are chatting about weekend plans, and Lucas suggests they spend a day exploring the city together.

Lucas: У вас є плани на цю суботу?
(Do you have plans this Saturday?)

Sofia: Нічого конкретного. У вас є ідеї?
(Nothing fixed. Do you have something in mind?)

Lucas: Так, я думав/думала, що ми могли б прогулятися центром, а потім пообідати десь. Вам це подобається?
(Yes, I was thinking we could explore downtown and then have dinner somewhere. Would you like that?)

Sofia: Я б із задоволенням! Звучить як хороший план.
(I'd love to! Sounds like a good plan.)

Lucas: Ідеально, тоді зустрінемося о четвертій у парку.
(Perfect, then let's meet at four in the park.)

DEEPENING THE CONVERSATION: MOVING BEYOND SMALL TALK

Once you've navigated through small talk and feel a positive connection, it can be rewarding to steer the conversation toward more meaningful topics. Deepening the conversation allows you to learn more about the other person's interests, values, and personality, helping you both feel more connected. In this section, we'll go over phrases to guide the conversation smoothly from light-hearted to personal and also providing you with an example dialogue to illustrate the transition.

Phrases for Transitioning to Personal Topics

When moving beyond small talk, the key is to keep your questions open-ended, allowing the other person to share as much or as little as they feel comfortable with. Here are some phrases to help you transition into deeper topics without feeling abrupt or intrusive:

- **Що вас захоплює? – What's something you're passionate about?**
  (Example response: Я захоплююся фотографією. Мені подобається знімати унікальні моменти. – I'm passionate about photography. I love capturing unique moments.)

- **Як би ви описали ідеальний день? – How would you describe a perfect day?**
  (Example response: Для мене ідеальний день — це на пляжі, з друзями та гарною музикою. – For me, a perfect day would be at the beach, with friends and good music.)

- **Що ви найбільше цінуєте в житті?** – What do you value most in life?
  (Example response: Я дуже ціную чесність і хорошу дружбу. – I really value honesty and good friendships.)

- **Що надихає чи мотивує вас щодня?** – What inspires or motivates you each day?
  (Example response: Мої мрії та цілі мотивують мене. – My dreams and goals keep me motivated.)

- **Яка найкраща порада, яку ви отримували?** – What's the best advice you've received?
  (Example response: Хтось колись сказав мені насолоджуватися теперішнім і не надто турбуватися про майбутнє. – Someone once told me to enjoy the present and not worry so much about the future.)

These questions allow you to move from casual topics to subjects that reveal more about the other person's personality, goals, and outlook on life. By keeping the tone positive and open, you can establish a deeper, more engaging connection.

Example Dialogue: Gradually Deepening the Conversation

Here's a sample conversation between Alex and Isabel as they move from light topics to a more personal exchange.

Alex: Я радий/рада, що ми сьогодні зустрілися. Ви надаєте перевагу каві чи чаю?
(I'm glad we met today. Do you prefer coffee or tea?)

Isabel: Думаю, я надаю перевагу каві. Не можу почати день без чашки.
(I think I prefer coffee. I can't start the day without a cup.)

Alex: Я також, кава — це необхідність. Що вас захоплює?
(Me too, coffee is essential. What's something you're passionate about?)

Isabel: Я захоплююся музикою. Я багато років граю на гітарі і люблю складати пісні.
(I'm passionate about music. I've been playing guitar for years, and I love composing songs.)

Alex: Це звучить неймовірно. Музика має унікальну здатність об'єднувати нас. Як би ви описали ідеальний день?
(That sounds amazing. Music has a unique way of connecting us. How would you describe a perfect day?)

Isabel: Для мене ідеальний день — це у хатині в горах, з моєю гітарою та добрими друзями. А у вас?
(For me, a perfect day would be in a cabin in the mountains, with my guitar and good friends. And you?)

Alex: Думаю, для мене ідеальний день — це подорожі та відкриття нових місць. Мене надихає знайомство з різними культурами та спроби нових страв.
(I think a perfect day for me would be traveling and exploring new places. I'm inspired by learning about different cultures and trying different foods.)

Isabel: Це звучить так захоплююче. Яка найкраща порада, яку ви отримували?
(That sounds so exciting. What's the best advice you've received?)

Alex: Хтось колись сказав мені, що ми завжди повинні слідувати своїм мріям, незалежно від того, наскільки вони здаються складними.
(Someone once told me that we should always follow our dreams, no matter how difficult they seem.)

Through this conversation, Alex and Isabel smoothly transition from casual topics to ones that touch on personal values and dreams, creating a comfortable and authentic connection. Both share details that reveal something meaningful about themselves, deepening the exchange.

FLIRTING THROUGH TEXT AND SOCIAL MEDIA

In today's world, flirting often starts with a simple message. Texting and social media provide a casual and fun way to show interest and get to know someone better. Flirting through text allows you to express yourself playfully while keeping the conversation light and engaging. In this section, we'll cover essential phrases for complimenting someone and showing interest via text.

Phrases for Flirting and Showing Interest via Text

When it comes to texting, a thoughtful compliment or a playful comment can go a long way. Here are some key phrases to keep the tone friendly, flirty, and inviting:

- **Завжди приємно з вами спілкуватися. – It's always a pleasure talking to you.**
  (*Example: Завжди приємно з вами спілкуватися. Ви змушуєте мене усміхатися. – It's always a pleasure talking to you. You make me smile.*)

- **Ця фотографія нагадала мені про вас. – This picture made me think of you.**
  (*Example: Я побачив/побачила фотографію пляжу, і це нагадало мені про вас. – I saw a picture of the beach, and it made me think of you.*)

- **Я радий/рада, що ми почали спілкуватися.** – I'm glad we started talking.
  (Example: Я радий/рада, що ми почали спілкуватися. Ви дуже цікава людина. – I'm glad we started talking. You're a very interesting person.)

- **У вас чудове почуття гумору.** – You have an amazing sense of humor.
  (Example: Ви завжди змушуєте мене сміятися. У вас чудове почуття гумору. – You always make me laugh. You have an amazing sense of humor.)

- **У чому секрет вашої чарівності?** – What's the secret to being so charming?
  (Example: У чому секрет вашої чарівності? Ви постійно мене дивуєте. – What's the secret to being so charming? You never cease to surprise me.)

Each of these phrases lets you show genuine interest and admiration while keeping the conversation lighthearted. They allow the other person to feel appreciated and provide opportunities for them to respond playfully.

Example Text Conversation: Moving from Playful to Meaningful

To see how these phrases work in a conversation, let's look at an example text exchange between Danial and Lucy as they go from lighthearted banter to a deeper connection.

Daniel: Привіт, Люсі. Я побачив/побачила фотографію пляжу, і це нагадало мені про вас. Ви такий/така ж великий шанувальник моря, як здається?
(Hi, Lucy. I saw a picture of a beach, and it made me think of you. Are you as big of a fan of the sea as you seem?)

Lucy: Привіт, Даніель! Так, я великий/велика шанувальник моря. Я могла/міг би проводити там години. Ви надаєте перевагу пляжу чи горам?
(Hi, Daniel! Yes, I'm a total fan of the sea. I could spend hours there. Do you prefer the beach or the mountains?)

Daniel: Безперечно, я також люблю пляж. До речі, завжди приємно з вами спілкуватися.
(Definitely, I'm a beach person too. By the way, it's always a pleasure talking to you.)

Lucy: Дякую, Даніель. Ви змушуєте мене усміхатися. Чому ми зараз не на пляжі?
(Thank you, Daniel. You make me smile. Why aren't we at the beach right now?)

Daniel: Хороше запитання. Можливо, нам слід запланувати день на пляжі. Хоча мені потрібно спочатку дізнатися секрет вашої чарівності.
(Good question. Maybe we should plan a beach day. Although I'd have to figure out the secret to being as charming as you first.)

Lucy: Ха-ха, ніякого секрету немає. Ви просто повинні насолоджуватися моментом. Хотіли б щось зробити цими вихідними?
(Haha, there's no secret. You just have to enjoy the moment. Would you like to do something this weekend?)

In this conversation, Daniel and Lucy smoothly move from playful teasing to suggesting a potential plan to meet up. Daniel's compliments are sincere yet light, and Lucy responds with humor, keeping the tone flirty and fun. They gradually introduce the idea of spending time together, transitioning from a text exchange to possibly meeting in person.

HANDLING AWKWARD MOMENTS AND MISUNDERSTANDINGS

Awkward moments and misunderstandings are a natural part of any conversation, especially when navigating a language barrier. When flirting in Ukrainian, these moments don't have to derail the conversation—in fact, they can even be an opportunity to show grace, patience, and a sense of humor. In this section, we'll cover polite phrases for clarifying misunderstandings and provide an example dialogue demonstrating how to recover from an awkward moment.

Phrases for Clarifying Misunderstandings Politely

Whether it's a language mix-up or a simple misunderstanding, addressing awkward moments with kindness and humor can help diffuse tension and keep the conversation moving. Here are some helpful phrases to handle misunderstandings gracefully:

- **Вибач, здається, я тебе неправильно зрозумів/зрозуміла. – Sorry, I think I didn't understand you well.**
  (*Example: Вибач, здається, я тебе неправильно зрозумів/зрозуміла. Можеш пояснити ще раз? – Sorry, I think I didn't understand you well. Could you explain it again?*)

- **Це те, що ти мав/мала на увазі? – Is that what you meant?**
  (*Example: То це те, що ти мав/мала на увазі? – So, is that what you meant?*)

- **Вибач, я не хотів/хотіла це сказати. – Sorry, I didn't mean to say that.**
  (Example: Вибач, я не хотів/хотіла це сказати. Сподіваюся, я тебе не образив/образила. – Sorry, I didn't mean to say that. I hope I didn't offend you.)

- **Думаю, у нас було невелике непорозуміння. – I think we had a little misunderstanding.**
  (Example: Думаю, у нас було невелике непорозуміння. Я мав/мала на увазі щось інше. – I think we had a little misunderstanding. I meant something different.)

- **Я не впевнений/впевнена, чи правильно зрозумів/зрозуміла. Можеш повторити? – I'm not sure I understood correctly. Could you repeat it?**
  (Example: Я не впевнений/впевнена, чи правильно зрозумів/зрозуміла. Можеш повторити повільніше? – I'm not sure I understood correctly. Could you repeat it more slowly?)

Using these phrases lets the other person know you're listening and want to clarify any confusion. This approach shows respect and an openness to communication, which can strengthen the bond between you.

Example Dialogue: Gracefully Recovering from a Misunderstanding

Here's an example conversation between Mike and Ana as they navigate a small misunderstanding. Notice how they use polite phrases to clarify and keep the conversation light.

Mike: Отже, хотів/хотіла б піти подивитися той бойовик цими вихідними?
(So, would you like to go see that action movie this weekend?)

Ana: О, я думав/думала, що тобі не подобаються бойовики.
(Oh, I thought you didn't like action movies.)

Mike: Вибач, здається, я раніше не дуже добре висловився/висловилася. Мені подобається їх дивитися, коли компанія гарна.
(Sorry, I think I didn't express myself well before. I like watching them when the company is good.)

Ana: Ха-ха, зрозуміло. Як щодо суботи?
(Haha, I see. So, how about Saturday?)

Mike: Ідеально. І вибач, якщо було якесь непорозуміння.
(Perfect. And sorry if there was any misunderstanding.)

Ana: Не переймайся, це дрібниці. Таке трапляється, особливо коли ми швидко говоримо.
(Don't worry, it's nothing. It happens sometimes, especially when we talk quickly.)

In this dialogue, Mike and Ana handle the misunderstanding with patience and humor. Mike clarifies his intent without over-apologizing, and Ana reassures him that it's not an issue. This approach maintains a relaxed and friendly tone, helping both feel comfortable.

TALKING ABOUT HOBBIES AND INTERESTS

Discussing hobbies and interests is a great way to get to know someone on a deeper level and discover shared passions. When you bring up topics like music, books, or favorite activities, you create a fun and engaging conversation that lets both people share a bit about what makes them unique. In this section, we'll cover essential vocabulary and phrases for talking about personal interests and also provide an example dialogue.

Vocabulary and Phrases for Discussing Hobbies

To start, here are some useful words and phrases to help you discuss common hobbies and personal interests. These can be used to ask about someone's hobbies or to share a bit about your own.

- **Я люблю живу музику. – I love live music.**
  (*Example*: Я люблю живу музику; я завжди шукаю нові концерти. – *I love live music; I'm always looking for new concerts.*)

- **Ти часто читаєш книги? – Do you read books often?**
  (*Example*: Ти часто читаєш книги? Я зараз читаю одну про історію. – *Do you read books often? I'm reading one about history right now.*)

- **Мені дуже подобається подорожувати і відкривати нові місця. – I really enjoy traveling and discovering new places.**
  (Example: Подорожі — це одне з моїх захоплень. Мені подобається знайомитися з новими культурами та пробувати різні страви. – Traveling is one of my passions. I enjoy experiencing new cultures and trying different foods.)

- **Тобі подобається займатися спортом? – Do you like playing sports?**
  (Example: Так, я граю в теніс і дуже люблю бігати. – Yes, I play tennis, and I really enjoy running.)

- **У тебе є улюблене хобі? – Do you have a favorite hobby?**
  (Example: Моє улюблене хобі — малювання. Це мене дуже розслабляє. – My favorite hobby is painting. It really relaxes me.)

These phrases can be easily adapted to fit the flow of your conversation. By using questions and statements that relate to the other person's interests, you show genuine curiosity and open the door for them to share what they're passionate about.

Example Dialogue: Discussing Hobbies and Interests

Here's a sample conversation between Sara and Daniel as they discuss their hobbies and find common interests. Notice how they use open-ended questions to keep the conversation flowing naturally.

Sara: Привіт, Даніель. Ти казав, що любиш музику. Тобі подобається іноді ходити на концерти?
(Hi, Daniel. You mentioned that you like music. Do you like going to concerts now and then?)

Daniel: Так, я люблю живу музику. Я завжди шукаю нові концерти. А ти?
(Yes, I love live music. I'm always looking for new concerts to see. Do you, too?)

Sara: Так, я це люблю. Я ходив/ходила на один минулого місяця, і це було неймовірно. Мені також подобається читати; а тобі?
(Yes, I love it. I went to one last month, and it was amazing. I also enjoy reading; what about you?)

Daniel: Мені подобається читати, але все залежить від теми. Останнім часом я читаю про подорожі. Мене захоплює відкриття нових місць.
(I like reading, but it depends on the topic. Lately, I've been reading about travel. I'm passionate about discovering new places.)

Sara: Який збіг! Подорожі — це теж одне з моїх захоплень. Яке останнє місце ти відвідав/відвідала?
(What a coincidence! Traveling is one of my passions, too. What's the last place you visited?)

Daniel: Я був/була в Перу минулого року. Це був неймовірний досвід. Є місце, куди ти завжди хотів/хотіла поїхати?
(I was in Peru last year. It was an incredible experience. Is there a place you've always wanted to go?)

In this conversation, Sara and Daniel move smoothly between different topics, discovering shared interests along the way. By asking each other about their hobbies and experiences, they're able to create a lively, meaningful dialogue where both feel engaged and appreciated.

NAVIGATING EMOTIONAL CONVERSATIONS

As you build a connection with someone, emotional conversations naturally become part of the journey. Discussing feelings, expectations, or boundaries can deepen your relationship and help establish mutual respect and understanding. However, navigating these topics requires sensitivity, respect, and open communication. In this section, we'll explore essential phrases for expressing emotions in Ukrainian and provide you with an example dialogue about relationship expectations or setting boundaries.

Phrases for Expressing Feelings

Using thoughtful, sincere language to express emotions helps create a comfortable environment where both people feel understood and valued. Here are some phrases that can help you communicate feelings in an open and respectful way:

- **З тобою мені дуже комфортно.** – You make me feel very comfortable.
  (Example: З тобою мені дуже комфортно, наче я можу бути собою. – You make me feel very comfortable, as if I can be myself.)

- **Я ціную, що ми можемо говорити щиро.** – I appreciate that we can talk honestly.
  (Example: Я ціную, що ми можемо говорити щиро про наші почуття. – I appreciate that we can talk honestly about our feelings.)

- **Мені подобається, що ти такий/така відкритий/відкрита зі мною. – I like that you're so open with me.**
  (*Example: Мені подобається, що ти такий/така відкритий/відкрита зі мною; це змушує мене відчувати, що ми стаємо ближчими. – I like that you're so open with me; it makes me feel closer to you.*)

- **Я відчуваю сильний зв'язок із тобою. – I feel very connected to you.**
  (*Example: Кожного разу, коли ми розмовляємо, я відчуваю сильний зв'язок із тобою. – Every time we talk, I feel very connected to you.*)

- **Для мене важливо, щоб у нас була хороша комунікація. – It's important to me that we have good communication.**
  (*Example: Для мене важливо, щоб у нас була хороша комунікація, щоб ми могли краще розуміти одне одного. – It's important to me that we have good communication so we can understand each other better.*)

Using these phrases shows vulnerability, helping to create a trusting atmosphere where both people feel comfortable sharing openly.

Example Dialogue: Discussing Relationship Expectations

Here's an example conversation between Carla and Andrew as they discuss their relationship expectations. They express their feelings and thoughts on communication and boundaries, ensuring that both feel heard and understood.

Carla: Привіт, Ендрю. Я хотів/хотіла поговорити з тобою про те, як ми почуваємося в цих стосунках.
(Hi, Andrew. I wanted to talk with you about how we're feeling in this relationship.)

Andrew: Звичайно, Карла. Я також ціную, що ми можемо говорити щиро про ці речі.
(Of course, Carla. I also appreciate that we can talk honestly about these things.)

Carla: Для мене важливо мати хорошу комунікацію. З тобою мені дуже комфортно, і я хочу, щоб ми завжди могли так говорити.
(For me, it's important to have good communication. You make me feel very comfortable, and I want us to always be able to talk like this.)

Andrew: Повністю згоден/згодна. Мені подобається, що ти такий/така відкритий/відкрита зі мною. Мені також цікаво дізнатися, чи є у тебе якісь конкретні очікування від наших стосунків.
(I completely agree. I like that you're so open with me. I'd also like to know if you have any specific expectations for our relationship.)

Carla: Я думаю, моє головне очікування — це те, що ми будемо підтримувати одне одного та поважати наші межі.
(I think my main expectation is that we can support each other and respect our boundaries.)

Andrew: Це також дуже важливо для мене. Я ціную, що ти так чітко говориш про свої почуття і очікування.
(That's very important to me too. I appreciate that you're so clear about how you feel and what you expect.)

In this conversation, Carla and Andrew express their feelings and expectations in a way that strengthens their connection. By actively listening and responding with understanding, they create an environment where both feel respected and supported.

CHAPTER SIX:
COMPLIMENTS AND RESPONSES

COMPLIMENTS ON APPEARANCE: MAKING A GREAT FIRST IMPRESSION

Giving a genuine compliment about someone's appearance can make them feel noticed and appreciated. In Ukrainian, compliments can range from lighthearted to deeply sincere, and knowing when and how to deliver them can greatly enhance your conversational skills. In this section, we will explore commonly used phrases, how to strike a balance between sincerity and subtlety, and tips for tailoring compliments to different contexts.

Common Phrases for Complimenting Appearance

Here are some go-to phrases for complimenting someone's appearance in Ukrainian:

- **Ти сьогодні виглядаєш чудово.** – You look amazing today.
  (*Example:* Ти сьогодні виглядаєш чудово; цей колір ідеально тобі пасує. – *You look amazing today; that color suits you perfectly.*)

- **У тебе гарні очі.** – You have beautiful eyes.
  (*Example:* Я завжди вважав/вважала, що у тебе гарні очі. – *I've always thought you have beautiful eyes.*)

- **Мені подобається твоя усмішка.** – I love your smile.
  (*Example:* Мені подобається твоя усмішка; вона освітлює кімнату. – *I love your smile; it lights up the room.*)

- **Ти виглядаєш дуже елегантно. – You look very elegant.**
  (Example: Ти сьогодні виглядаєш дуже елегантно; наче готовий/готова до особливої нагоди. – You look very elegant today; you seem ready for a special occasion.)

- **Ця зачіска тобі дуже пасує. – That hairstyle looks great on you.**
  (Example: Ця зачіска тобі дуже пасує; ти виглядаєш сяючою/сяючим. – That hairstyle looks great on you; it makes you look radiant.)

Balancing Sincerity and Subtlety

Compliments are most effective when they come across as genuine and appropriate for the situation. Striking a balance between being sincere and subtle helps prevent your words from seeming forced or overly intense.

- **Be Genuine:** Always give compliments that you truly mean. If you don't feel the sentiment behind your words, it's likely that the other person will notice.

- **Keep It Simple:** Especially when meeting someone for the first time, choose compliments that are simple and avoid embellishments. For instance, saying *"Ти виглядаєш чудово"* (You look great) feels casual and warm, while *"Твоя краса залишає мене без слів"* (Your beauty leaves me speechless) might be too much for a first encounter.

- **Consider the Setting:** A compliment at a casual meetup should differ from one at a formal event. For example, *"Ти виглядаєш дуже елегантно"* is more suited for a formal dinner, while *"Мені подобається твій стиль"* (I like your style) works well for a casual gathering.

Tips for Tailoring Compliments to the Context

1. **Casual Settings:** When meeting someone at a party, café, or other informal setting, keep your compliments light and friendly.

    - **Мені дуже подобається твоя сорочка; у неї крутий дизайн.** – I really like your shirt; it has a cool design.

    - **Цей колір тобі дуже пасує, ти виглядаєш дуже життєрадісно.** – That color looks great on you, it makes you look very lively.

2. **Formal Settings:** In a more formal environment, compliments should be polished and respectful.

    - **Ти сьогодні виглядаєш дуже вишукано.** – You look very sophisticated tonight.

    - **Ця куртка дуже елегантна; вона ідеально тобі пасує.** – That jacket is very elegant; it fits you perfectly.

3. **Cultural Awareness:** It's essential to be mindful of how compliments might be received in Ukrainian culture. In some regions, compliments about appearance are common and welcomed, while in others, they might be taken more seriously. Pay attention to non-verbal cues and how the other person responds to adjust your approach as needed.

COMPLIMENTS ON PERSONALITY: GOING BEYOND LOOKS

While compliments on appearance are often appreciated, going a step further by highlighting someone's personality can build deeper rapport and create a more meaningful connection. Compliments that recognize unique traits show that you are paying attention to who the person truly is, not just how they look. In this section, we'll explore common phrases to compliment someone's personality in Ukrainian and when and how to use them to deepen your bond.

Common Phrases for Complimenting Personality

Here are some key phrases to express admiration for someone's character or traits:

- **Мені подобається твоє почуття гумору.** – I love your sense of humor.
  (Example: Мені подобається твоє почуття гумору; ти завжди знаєш, як мене розсмішити. – I love your sense of humor; you always know how to make me laugh.)

- **Ти дуже цікава людина.** – You're a very interesting person.
  (Example: Кожного разу, коли ми розмовляємо, я розумію, що ти дуже цікава людина. – Every time we talk, I realize you're a very interesting person.)

- **У тебе особливий погляд на життя, який надихає мене.** – You have a way of looking at life that inspires me.
  (Example: У тебе особливий погляд на життя, який надихає мене дивитися на речі по-іншому. – You have a way of looking at life that inspires me to see things differently.)

- **Я захоплююся тим, наскільки ти добрий/добра до інших.** – I admire how kind you are to others.
  (Example: Я захоплююся тим, наскільки ти добрий/добра до інших; це рідкісна якість. – I admire how kind you are to others; it's a rare quality.)

- **Ти дуже щирий/щира, і це те, що я дуже ціную.** – You're very genuine, and that's something I value a lot.
  (Example: Ти дуже щирий/щира, і це те, що я дуже ціную в людях. – You're very genuine, and that's something I value a lot in a person.)

When and How to Use Personality-Based Compliments

Giving a compliment on someone's personality can be particularly powerful in building a connection. Here's how to effectively use these types of compliments:

1. **Be Observant:** Compliment specific traits you've noticed during your interactions. This shows that you're genuinely paying attention, making your words more meaningful.

   - Example: If your conversation partner tells funny stories or makes witty remarks, saying *"Мені подобається твоє почуття гумору"* feels personal and relevant.

2. **Choose the Right Moment:** Deliver personality-based compliments when the conversation naturally allows for it. This might be after someone shares a story, offers advice, or exhibits a quality you admire.

   - Example: After they talk about volunteering or helping someone, you could say *"Я захоплююся тим, наскільки ти добрий/добра до інших"*.

3. **Balance and Sincerity:** Ensure your compliments sound sincere and are balanced with other conversation topics. Avoid giving too many compliments in one go, as it may feel overwhelming or insincere.

4. **Use Follow-Up Questions:** Compliments on personality can be great conversation starters. Follow them up with questions to encourage the other person to talk more about themselves.

   - Example: After saying *"Ти дуже цікава людина"*, you could add *"Що тебе зацікавило в цій темі?"* (What got you interested in that topic?).

HOW TO ACCEPT COMPLIMENTS GRACEFULLY

Receiving compliments can sometimes be as challenging as giving them, especially when the compliments are unexpected or make you feel self-conscious. In Ukrainian culture, accepting compliments with poise shows not only gratitude but also confidence and respect for the person giving them. In this section, we'll explore how to respond to compliments gracefully, including specific phrases, tips on maintaining sincerity, and the importance of body language.

Phrases for Accepting Compliments

When someone gives you a compliment, it's essential to acknowledge it in a way that feels warm and sincere. Here are some common responses in Ukrainian to express gratitude:

- **Дякую, ти дуже добрий/добра.** – Thank you, you're very kind.
  (*Example: Дякую, ти дуже добрий/добра, що це сказав/сказала. – Thank you, you're very kind for saying that.*)

- **Ти змушуєш мене червоніти.** – You're making me blush.
  (*Example: Ого, ти змушуєш мене червоніти своїми словами. – Wow, you're making me blush with your words.*)

- **Як мило з твого боку.** – How sweet of you.
  (*Example: Як мило з твого боку, що ти це помітив/помітила. – How sweet of you to notice that.*)

- **Я дуже це ціную. – I appreciate it a lot.**
  (*Example:* Дякую, я дуже це ціную; це багато для мене значить. – *Thank you, I appreciate it a lot; it means a lot to me.*)

- **Радий/рада, що ти так вважаєш. – I'm glad you think so.**
  (*Example:* Радий/рада, що ти так вважаєш; я завжди намагаюся робити все найкраще. – *I'm glad you think so; I always try to do my best.*)

Tips for Accepting Compliments with Grace

Accepting compliments may feel awkward at times, but with the right approach, you can respond in a way that is both gracious and confident. Here are some tips:

1. **Express Genuine Gratitude:** Always respond with a "thank you" to acknowledge the compliment. This basic courtesy shows that you appreciate the effort someone made to recognize something positive about you.

   - Example: *"Дякую, я радий/рада, що тобі це подобається."* – Thank you, I'm glad you like it.

2. **Add a Personal Touch:** If you feel comfortable, add a brief comment that makes your response more personal. This could be something like *"Я радий/рада, що ти це помітив/помітила"* (I'm glad you noticed) or *"Мені приємно, що тобі це подобається"* (It makes me happy that you like it).

3. **Avoid Dismissive Responses:** It can be tempting to downplay a compliment out of modesty, but responses like "Oh, it's nothing" or "No, not really" can come across as rude or dismissive. Accepting a compliment doesn't mean you're being arrogant; it simply shows that you respect the other person's opinion.

    - Replace *"О, це не так вже й важливо"* (Oh, it's not that big of a deal) with *"Дякую, ти дуже добрий/добра"* (Thank you, you're very kind).

4. **Use Body Language:** Non-verbal cues like smiling, maintaining eye contact, and a slight nod can convey sincerity and warmth when accepting a compliment. These gestures reinforce your spoken response and show that you truly appreciate the kind words.

5. **Stay Confident:** Accepting a compliment confidently shows that you value yourself and the effort or trait being praised. If someone tells you that your presentation was excellent, for instance, respond with *"Дякую, я багато працював/працювала над цим"* (Thank you, I worked hard on it) to show pride in your efforts.

COMPLIMENTS FOR SPECIFIC INTERESTS AND ACHIEVEMENTS

Giving compliments that highlight someone's interests or achievements can make conversations more meaningful and personal. These types of compliments show that you're paying attention to what the other person is passionate about and that you genuinely admire their dedication or skills.

Phrases for Complimenting Interests and Achievements

Here are some key phrases in Ukrainian that you can use to compliment someone's hobbies and achievements:

- **У тебе великий талант до фотографії.** – You have a great talent for photography.
  (*Example: У тебе великий талант до фотографії; твої фотографії завжди передають особливі моменти. – You have a great talent for photography; your photos always capture special moments.*)

- **Я захоплююся твоєю відданістю роботі.** – I admire your dedication to work.
  (*Example: Я захоплююся твоєю відданістю роботі; це надихає бачити, наскільки ти відданий/віддана. – I admire your dedication to work; it's inspiring to see how committed you are.*)

- **Ти дуже креативний/креативна; твої ідеї завжди мене дивують.** – You're very creative; your ideas always surprise me.
  (Example: Ти дуже креативний/креативна; твої ідеї та рішення завжди мене дивують. – You're very creative; your ideas and solutions always surprise me.)

- **Твоя майстерність гри на піаніно вражає.** – Your ability to play the piano is impressive.
  (Example: Твоя майстерність гри на піаніно вражає; слухати тебе — справжнє задоволення. – Your ability to play the piano is impressive; it's a pleasure to listen to you.)

- **Твоя відданість своїм захопленням викликає захоплення.** – You have an admirable dedication to your hobbies.
  (Example: Твоя відданість своїм захопленням викликає захоплення; це показує велику пристрасть. – You have an admirable dedication to your hobbies; that shows a lot of passion.)

When and How to Use These Compliments

Understanding when and how to use compliments about interests and achievements can help build stronger connections and show genuine interest. Here's how to make the most of these compliments:

1. **Observe and Listen:** Pay attention to what the other person shares about their hobbies, achievements, or passions. Use their cues as opportunities to offer a relevant compliment.

    - Example: If someone tells you about their recent marathon, you could say, *"Я захоплююся твоєю відданістю тренуванням; це вимагає багато дисципліни."* (I admire your dedication to training; that requires a lot of discipline.)

2. **Be Specific:** A specific compliment shows that you're truly paying attention and adds more weight to your words.

    - Instead of a generic, *"Ти дуже талановитий/талановита"* (You're very talented), try *"У тебе великий талант до фотографії; твої фотографії завжди розповідають історію."* (You have a great talent for photography; your photos always tell a story.)

3. **Choose the Right Moment:** Compliments about achievements are best given during or after a conversation about the topic. Avoid delivering them out of context, as they may seem forced or insincere.

    - Example: If your colleague shares a successful project result, you could say, *"Твоя презентація була чудова; я захоплююся твоєю відданістю роботі."* (Your presentation was excellent; I admire your dedication to work.)

4. **Express Genuine Interest:** Follow up your compliment with a question or statement that shows you want to learn more. This can encourage the other person to share more about their interests or achievements.

    - Example: *"У тебе великий талант до фотографії. Як ти почав/почала захоплюватися цим?"* (You have a great talent for photography. How did you start with this passion?)

FLIRTING WITH QUESTIONS: KEEPING THE CONVERSATION GOING

Once you've broken the ice with a greeting and perhaps a compliment, the next challenge is keeping the conversation flowing. One of the best ways to do this is by asking engaging, thoughtful questions that show genuine interest in the other person. The right questions not only encourage the other person to open up but also allow you to showcase your curiosity, humor, and charm.

In Ukrainian, as in any language, how you ask a question can signal interest and even flirtation. In this section, you'll learn how to use questions to continue conversations, ranging from casual to playful, and how to use follow-up questions to keep the momentum going.

Asking Engaging Questions to Show Interest

A great way to show someone that you're interested in them is to ask about their life, hobbies, and preferences. These questions invite the other person to talk about themselves, which can help build a connection. They also give you a chance to discover shared interests that could keep the conversation going naturally.

Here are some examples of basic, yet effective, questions to ask when you're getting to know someone:

- **Що ти робиш у свій вільний час?**
  (What do you do in your free time?)

  This is an open-ended question that gives the other person the opportunity to talk about their hobbies, passions, or activities they enjoy. It's also a great way to discover shared interests, which can help deepen the conversation.

- **Який твій улюблений фільм?**
  (What's your favorite movie?)

  Asking about someone's favorite movie or type of film can lead to a lively discussion, especially if you share similar tastes. It's also a lighthearted question that can open the door to a more relaxed and fun conversation.

- **У тебе є якісь захоплення?**
  (Do you have any hobbies?)

  Asking about hobbies is another good way to keep the conversation going, as it allows the person to share what they're passionate about outside of work or daily routines.

- **Яку музику ти любиш?**
  (What kind of music do you like?)

  Music is a universal topic that many people love to talk about. Asking this question can help you find common ground and spark a fun exchange about favorite bands, concerts, or even music-related experiences.

By asking these kinds of questions, you're giving the other person the chance to talk about themselves, which is a great way to keep the conversation engaging. These questions also signal that you're genuinely interested in learning more about who they are.

Keeping the Conversation Playful

Flirting often involves a playful back-and-forth that adds excitement to the interaction. Playful questions can introduce humor and keep the conversation light while still showing interest. These types of questions allow you to tease the other person in a fun and friendly way, helping to create a sense of connection.

Here are some playful questions you can use to add a little flirtatious energy to your conversation:

- **Якби ти був/була супергероєм, яку силу ти мав/мала б?**
  (If you were a superhero, what power would you have?)

  This fun, imaginative question invites the other person to think outside the box and share something creative about themselves. It's a playful way to keep the conversation going, and their answer can lead to more teasing and lighthearted banter.

- **Ти загубився/загубилася? Бо рай далеко звідси.**
  (Are you lost? Because heaven is far from here.)

  This classic playful line is cheeky and fun. It's a bold way to add a little humor to the conversation while also giving a compliment. The key here is in the delivery—make sure to smile and keep your tone light.

- **Якби ти міг/могла повечеряти з будь-ким у світі, хто б це був?**
  (If you could have dinner with anyone in the world, who would it be?)

  This question is playful yet insightful. It encourages the other person to think about their role models or favorite celebrities, which can lead to an interesting discussion about who inspires them or who they admire.

- **Яке твоє ідеальне місце для відпочинку?**
  (What's your ideal vacation spot?)

  Asking about vacation spots not only keeps the conversation light but also lets you explore the person's preferences for adventure or relaxation. You can share stories about travel, or even suggest potential future trips as the conversation progresses.

How to Follow Up and Keep the Momentum

Once you've asked an engaging or playful question, it's important to follow up on their response to keep the conversation flowing. The best follow-up questions dig a little deeper into what the other person has shared, showing that you're listening and genuinely interested.

For example, if they respond to *"Що ти робиш у свій вільний час?"* by saying they enjoy painting, you could follow up with questions like:

- **Як цікаво! Скільки часу ти малюєш?**
  (How interesting! How long have you been painting?)

- **Тобі подобається малювати пейзажі чи портрети?**
  (Do you like painting landscapes or portraits?)

Follow-up questions like these show that you're paying attention to the details of the conversation and encourage the other person to share even more. They also allow you to explore topics that go beyond surface-level conversation, making the interaction more meaningful.

Another key tip is to listen for opportunities to add a playful twist to their responses. For example, if they mention that their favorite movie is a superhero film, you could follow up with something like:

- **То тобі подобаються супергерої? Можливо, ти сам/сама супергерой, а я просто ще цього не знаю.**
  (So, you like superheroes? Maybe you're one yourself, and I just don't know it yet.)

This playful banter keeps the tone light and helps maintain the flirtatious vibe of the conversation.

CHAPTER SEVEN:
HANDLING REJECTION

UNDERSTANDING REJECTION: THE REALITY OF DATING

Rejection is an inevitable part of dating and flirting, no matter how confident, charming, or well-prepared someone may be. While being turned down can be disappointing and sometimes even painful, understanding why rejection happens and reframing it as a learning experience can help individuals grow, build resilience, and continue to engage in meaningful relationships with confidence. In this section, we'll delve into the psychology behind rejection, explore why it occurs, and highlight why it should never be taken as a measure of personal worth.

The Nature of Rejection in Dating

Rejection is a natural aspect of any social interaction involving human emotions and preferences. It happens for a multitude of reasons, many of which are beyond one's control. These reasons can range from simple compatibility issues to timing and personal circumstances. It is important to remember that rejection often says more about the preferences or situation of the other person than it does about the individual being rejected.

Even the most confident, attractive, and successful individuals face rejection. The reality is, not everyone will click with everyone else, and that is perfectly okay. Viewing rejection as an expected part of the dating process can help manage feelings of disappointment and foster a healthier approach to relationships.

Psychological Reasons Behind Rejection

Understanding the psychology behind rejection can help demystify the experience and make it easier to accept. Here are some common psychological reasons why rejection occurs:

1. **Personal Preferences and Compatibility:** Everyone has unique preferences, interests, and values that play a significant role in their choice of a partner. Sometimes, these differences become apparent early on, leading to a polite decline of further interaction.

2. **Emotional Readiness:** Sometimes, rejection happens because the other person may not be in the right emotional place for a relationship. This could be due to past experiences, personal struggles, or simply not being ready for a new connection.

3. **Chemistry and Attraction:** There are elements of attraction and chemistry that are intangible and often difficult to define. If these elements are missing, the connection may not progress further, even if both parties are kind and compatible in other ways.

4. **Misaligned Intentions:** Rejection can also occur when people have different intentions or expectations from the interaction. For example, one person may be looking for a serious relationship, while the other is interested in something more casual.

Reframing Rejection as an Opportunity for Growth

Experiencing rejection can feel like a blow to self-esteem, but it doesn't have to be. Reframing the experience as a valuable learning opportunity can transform the way it is perceived. Here's how:

- **Building Resilience:** Each rejection helps build emotional strength. Learning to process disappointment and move forward with grace enhances one's resilience, making future interactions less intimidating.

- **Gaining Insight:** Reflecting on the situation can offer insights into one's approach, communication style, or choice of partners. While it's crucial not to overanalyze, constructive reflection can help improve future experiences.

- **Understanding Personal Growth:** Rejection can serve as a reminder that self-worth should not be contingent on external validation. It encourages individuals to focus on their strengths, personal goals, and well-being, ensuring they remain confident and centered, regardless of the outcome.

RESPONDING WITH GRACE AND POSITIVITY

Rejection, while challenging, is an essential aspect of dating and social interactions. Responding with grace and positivity not only preserves one's dignity but can leave a lasting, positive impression on the other person. Knowing how to handle rejection in a composed manner helps foster self-respect and ensures that interactions remain respectful and pleasant. In this section, we'll explore strategies and examples for responding to rejection in Ukrainian, the importance of not taking it personally, and tips on maintaining composure.

The Importance of Responding Gracefully

Responding gracefully to rejection is a reflection of maturity and emotional intelligence. It shows that you respect the other person's decision and value your own self-worth. Here's why this approach matters:

- **Maintains Your Dignity:** A positive response helps you maintain your self-respect and shows that you can handle challenges maturely.

- **Leaves a Good Impression:** Even if a romantic connection doesn't work out, your composed reaction can leave a lasting, favorable impression on the other person.

- **Promotes Personal Growth:** Responding gracefully reinforces your resilience and ability to manage difficult emotions constructively.

Sample Responses to Rejection

When faced with rejection, it's essential to choose your words carefully to express understanding and gratitude. Here are some sample phrases in Ukrainian that can help you respond in a positive and respectful manner:

- **Дякую за вашу чесність, я це ціную.**
  (Thank you for your honesty, I appreciate it.)

  This response shows that you value transparency and are respectful of their feelings.

- **Я розумію і поважаю ваше рішення. Було приємно познайомитися.**
  (I understand and respect your decision. It was a pleasure meeting you.)

  This acknowledges their choice and leaves the interaction on a kind note.

- **Бажаю вам усього найкращого. Бережіть себе.**
  (I wish you all the best. Take care.)

  A brief, positive send-off that shows maturity and goodwill.

- **Дякую, що сказали це так делікатно. Я ціную вашу відвертість.**
  (Thank you for telling me in such a considerate way. I appreciate your candor.)

  This can be used when the rejection is expressed thoughtfully and shows that you recognize their effort.

Avoiding Defensive or Negative Reactions

When emotions run high, it can be tempting to respond defensively or with frustration. However, doing so can damage your self-esteem and reputation. Here's how to avoid negative reactions:

- **Take a Breath Before Responding:** Give yourself a moment to process your emotions before you respond. A pause can prevent impulsive or defensive replies.

- **Focus on Understanding, Not Justifying:** Remember that rejection is often due to compatibility, preferences, or timing. Avoid justifying yourself or questioning the other person's decision.

- **Keep It Short and Positive:** A concise, positive response is better than an extended explanation or argument.

Tips for Staying Composed

1. **Remind Yourself That It's Not Personal:** Rejection often has more to do with the other person's feelings, preferences, or circumstances than with you. Keeping this in mind can help reduce the sting of rejection.

2. **Practice Kindness Toward Yourself:** After responding, engage in a self-care activity that uplifts you. Whether it's spending time with friends, enjoying a favorite hobby, or reflecting on positive affirmations, self-care helps maintain your well-being.

3. **Use Humor If Appropriate:** Sometimes, adding light humor can help diffuse tension and show that you can take the situation in stride. For example, *"Ну що ж, я прийму нагороду за участь"* (Well, I'll take the participation award).

MAINTAINING SELF-CONFIDENCE POST-REJECTION

Rejection, while challenging, doesn't have to diminish your self-confidence or define your self-worth. In fact, it can be an opportunity to reaffirm your value and develop resilience. This section will guide you on how to maintain and rebuild self-confidence after facing rejection, emphasizing the importance of a positive mindset, self-care, and affirmations.

Tips for Maintaining a Positive Mindset

Maintaining a positive mindset post-rejection starts with shifting your perspective and focusing on what truly matters: your personal growth, well-being, and confidence. Here are some tips to help you stay positive:

1. **Acknowledge Your Emotions:** It's normal to feel disappointed or disheartened after rejection. Allow yourself to experience these emotions without judgment. Recognizing your feelings is the first step toward processing them healthily.

2. **Reframe the Experience:** View rejection as a sign that the match wasn't right, rather than a reflection of your worth. Tell yourself, *"Якщо це не для мене, то прийде щось краще"* (If it wasn't for me, something better will come).

3. **Focus on Your Strengths:** Remind yourself of your positive qualities and achievements. Reflect on what makes you unique and valuable. This can help redirect your thoughts from what didn't work out to what you appreciate about yourself.

4. **Avoid Overgeneralizing:** It's easy to think, "This always happens to me," but remember that one rejection does not mean a pattern. Challenge these negative thoughts by reminding yourself of times you felt confident and connected with others.

Affirmations to Reinforce Self-Worth

Affirmations are positive statements that help shift your mindset and reinforce confidence. Here are some affirmations in Ukrainian that can boost your self-esteem:

- **Я цінна/цінний і заслуговую на повагу.**
  (I am valuable and deserve respect.)

- **У мене є унікальні якості, які додають цінності моїм стосункам.**
  (I have unique qualities that bring value to my relationships.)

- **Кожен досвід, хороший чи поганий, допомагає мені зростати і вчитися.**
  (Every experience, good or bad, helps me grow and learn.)

- **Я вірю у свою здатність долати труднощі.**
  (I trust in my ability to overcome challenges.)

Say these affirmations to yourself daily or write them in a journal to internalize their meaning. By repeating positive affirmations, you reprogram your mind to believe in your inherent worth, even after difficult moments.

Self-Care and Activities to Reinforce Confidence

Self-care is an essential part of maintaining self-confidence. Here are some self-care practices and activities that can help reinforce your sense of self:

1. **Engage in Your Passions:** Pursue hobbies that bring you joy and fulfillment, whether it's painting, hiking, playing music, or cooking. Doing what you love can remind you of your abilities and talents.

2. **Connect with Supportive Friends:** Surround yourself with people who uplift and encourage you. Positive social interactions can help counteract feelings of inadequacy and remind you that you're appreciated.

3. **Set New Personal Goals:** Focus on personal development by setting achievable goals that excite and challenge you. These can be related to work, fitness, or creative projects. Achieving these goals will boost your self-esteem and prove that your worth is not tied to the opinions of others.

4. **Physical Activity and Health:** Exercise not only strengthens your body but also releases endorphins that improve your mood. A walk, yoga session, or workout can clear your mind and reset your focus.

5. **Mindfulness and Meditation:** Practice mindfulness to stay present and detach from negative thoughts. Meditation can help reduce stress and build inner peace, reinforcing your emotional resilience.

SETTING BOUNDARIES AND RESPECTING OTHERS' DECISIONS

One of the most important aspects of navigating social and romantic interactions is knowing when and how to set boundaries and respecting the decisions of others. Understanding when persistence is unwelcome and responding to rejection with grace helps build a positive reputation and maintains mutual respect. In this section, we'll explore how to handle rejection respectfully, differentiate between expressing disappointment and pressuring someone, and provide useful phrases to gracefully accept someone's decision.

The Importance of Setting Boundaries and Respecting Others

Boundaries are crucial for healthy interactions and demonstrate self-respect and consideration for others. When someone sets a boundary or communicates that they're not interested, it's essential to acknowledge their feelings without trying to change their mind. Respecting boundaries shows emotional intelligence and maturity and can even preserve a sense of friendship or civility in the future.

- **Recognizing Unwelcome Persistence:** Persistence can sometimes be seen as a positive quality, but there's a fine line between being persistent and disregarding someone's comfort. It's important to recognize the cues that indicate when persistence becomes unwelcome:

- **Verbal Indicators:** Phrases such as *"Я б вважав/вважала за краще не продовжувати це"* (I'd prefer not to continue with this) or *"Я не зацікавлений/зацікавлена"* (I'm not interested) should be respected immediately.

- **Non-Verbal Cues:** Pay attention to body language like avoiding eye contact, crossed arms, or stepping back. These signals often indicate discomfort or disinterest.

Expressing Disappointment vs. Pressuring Someone

There is a clear distinction between expressing disappointment and pressuring someone:

- **Expressing Disappointment:** It's natural to feel disappointed when someone doesn't reciprocate your interest. You can express this in a way that shows you accept their decision without trying to make them feel guilty. For instance, saying, *"Дякую за вашу чесність. Хоча я б хотів/хотіла іншу відповідь, я поважаю ваше рішення"* (Thank you for your honesty. Although I would have liked a different response, I respect your decision) acknowledges your feelings while affirming their choice.

- **Pressuring Someone:** On the other hand, phrases like *"Чому б вам не переглянути своє рішення?"* (Why don't you reconsider?) or *"Просто дайте мені шанс"* (Just give me a chance) can make the other person feel uncomfortable or trapped. These statements imply that their initial response is not valid or respected.

Phrases to Gracefully Accept Rejection

Here are some useful phrases in Ukrainian for gracefully accepting someone's decision:

- **Я розумію і поважаю ваше рішення, було приємно познайомитися.**
  (I understand and respect your decision, it was a pleasure meeting you.)

  This phrase expresses understanding and ends the conversation on a positive note.

- **Дякую за вашу чесність. Бажаю вам усього найкращого.**
  (Thank you for your honesty. I wish you the best.)

  A simple way to show appreciation for their openness and convey goodwill.

- **Я ціную, що ви сказали мені прямо. Гарного вам дня.**
  (I appreciate you telling me directly. Have a good day.)

  This response highlights your gratitude for their clarity and maintains dignity.

TURNING REJECTION INTO A POSITIVE EXPERIENCE

Rejection, while difficult to face, can be a powerful catalyst for personal and relational growth. It's natural to feel disheartened when things don't go as planned, but by viewing rejection through a different lens, it's possible to transform it from a source of discouragement into a valuable learning experience. This section will encourage you to see rejection as a stepping stone that fuels motivation, fosters resilience, and keeps you open to new opportunities.

Viewing Rejection as Growth, Not Failure

The way you choose to interpret rejection can shape your mindset and future interactions. Instead of seeing it as a reflection of your inadequacies, think of rejection as part of the process of discovering what aligns best with your goals and values.

- **Rejection as a Learning Tool:** Each interaction teaches you something new—whether about yourself, your approach, or what you want in a potential partner. When faced with rejection, ask yourself, *"Чого я можу навчитися з цього досвіду?"* (What can I learn from this experience?). This reflection helps turn a disappointing moment into a valuable insight.

- **Fostering Resilience:** Each time you experience rejection and choose to move forward, you strengthen your emotional resilience. This resilience is what allows you to approach future situations with confidence, knowing that setbacks are temporary and part of growth.

- **Refocusing Your Perspective:** Rejection often feels personal, but it's essential to recognize that it is frequently about compatibility rather than shortcomings. One missed opportunity can pave the way for a better-suited connection in the future.

Turning Rejection into Motivation

Using rejection as a source of motivation can lead to self-improvement and new possibilities. Here are some strategies to help shift your mindset:

- **Set New Goals:** Let rejection inspire you to set personal and social goals that excite you. This could mean trying out a new hobby, attending more social events, or improving your communication skills. These goals help you shift your focus from what didn't work out to what lies ahead.

- **Reframe the Narrative:** Change how you talk to yourself about rejection. Instead of saying, *"Я недостатньо хороший/хороша"* (I'm not good enough), try saying, *"Цей досвід навчив мене чогось цінного і допомагає мені зростати"* (This experience has taught me something valuable and is helping me grow).

- **Learn from Inspirational Stories:** Many successful individuals have faced rejection but used it as motivation to persevere. For example, renowned author Gabriel García Márquez received countless rejections for his early works before becoming a celebrated writer. His determination to continue writing and refining his craft paid off, showing that persistence and learning from setbacks can lead to success.

Staying Open to Future Opportunities

Fear of rejection can make you hesitant to put yourself out there again. However, staying open to new experiences is essential for growth and connection.

1. **Acknowledge the Fear, but Move Forward:** It's okay to feel nervous about facing rejection again. The key is to acknowledge the fear and take small steps forward despite it. Each attempt reinforces your confidence.

2. **Adopt a Growth Mindset:** Embrace the idea that every interaction, even if it ends in rejection, contributes to your personal development. Each experience builds your communication skills, emotional resilience, and understanding of what you want in relationships.

3. **Celebrate Small Wins:** Recognize and celebrate progress, no matter how small. For example, if you took the initiative to start a conversation or expressed your feelings clearly, these are successes in their own right.

MOVING FORWARD: EMBRACING NEW OPPORTUNITIES

Rejection is a natural part of the dating and social landscape, but it doesn't have to hold you back from future opportunities. In fact, the way you choose to move forward after facing rejection can define your confidence and readiness for new connections. This section will guide you on steps to re-enter the dating or social scene with optimism, emphasizing resilience and excitement for what lies ahead.

Steps to Re-Enter the Dating Scene with Positivity

Re-engaging with the dating world or social interactions after experiencing rejection can feel daunting. However, these steps can help you approach it with a fresh, positive mindset:

1. **Acknowledge Your Feelings:** Take a moment to recognize any lingering emotions from the rejection. It's important to validate how you felt but avoid dwelling on it. A phrase like *"Це був складний досвід, але я готовий/готова рухатися далі"* (It was a tough experience, but I'm ready to move forward) can be a helpful reminder of your resilience.

2. **Reflect on Your Strengths:** Remind yourself of what makes you unique and attractive. List your positive traits, whether it's your sense of humor, kindness, or ability to hold engaging conversations. This boosts your confidence and helps you walk into new situations with self-assurance.

3. **Reframe Rejection as Growth:** View past rejections as learning experiences that refine your approach and understanding of what you want. Think of it as practice that prepares you for better-suited connections. Say to yourself, *"Кожен крок наближає мене до потрібної людини"* (Each step brings me closer to the right person).

4. **Set Realistic Expectations:** Entering the dating or social scene without expecting immediate success can help reduce pressure. Instead of focusing on the outcome, aim to enjoy the experience of meeting new people.

5. **Stay Open and Curious:** Approach each new interaction with curiosity rather than anticipation. This mindset allows you to appreciate the person in front of you without the weight of expectations.

Tips for Practicing Resilience

Resilience is key to maintaining a positive attitude in the face of setbacks. Here's how to build and maintain resilience as you navigate new social opportunities:

- **Surround Yourself with Supportive People:** Lean on friends and family who uplift and encourage you. Positive interactions with those who know your worth can remind you that one rejection doesn't define you.

- **Maintain a Growth Mindset:** Embrace the idea that your social and dating skills can always improve. Each interaction, whether it leads to a connection or not, is part of a learning journey.

- **Practice Self-Compassion:** Be kind to yourself when things don't go as planned. Replace self-criticism with affirmations like *"Я вчуся і вдосконалююся щодня"* (I am learning and improving every day).

- **Celebrate Small Wins:** Acknowledge and celebrate small successes, like striking up a conversation or making someone smile. These moments reinforce your ability to connect and contribute to building your confidence.

Maintaining Excitement for New Connections

Staying excited about the possibility of new relationships or friendships keeps you motivated and optimistic. Here's how to maintain that excitement:

1. **Approach with an Open Mind:** Remind yourself that each person you meet has something unique to offer. This can make interactions feel fresh and interesting.

2. **Focus on Shared Interests:** When engaging with others, find common ground that excites you. Shared passions can make conversations more enjoyable and help establish a genuine connection.

3. **Stay Present:** Avoid overthinking the outcome of your interactions. Instead, enjoy the moment and be fully engaged. This not only makes you appear more confident but also helps you build a connection without added pressure.

CHAPTER EIGHT:
FUN QUIZZES & FLIRTING CHALLENGES

WHAT'S YOUR FLIRTING STYLE?

Flirting can take on many different forms, and understanding your natural style can make interactions more enjoyable and authentic. Whether you lean toward being playful, romantic, subtle, or direct, knowing how you express interest can help you navigate social situations with more confidence. In this section, you'll take a fun quiz to uncover your flirting style, learn how it aligns with Ukrainian culture, and receive personalized tips for enhancing your approach.

The Flirting Style Quiz

Answer the following questions to find out which flirting style best describes you. Choose the option that most closely aligns with your natural behavior:

1. When you see someone you're interested in, you typically:

    - A) Make eye contact and smile with a playful nod.
    - B) Start a conversation with a sincere compliment.
    - C) Drop subtle hints through your body language and words.
    - D) Walk up confidently and express your interest straightforwardly.

2. Your go-to conversation starter is:

- A) "Ти надаєш перевагу пляжу чи горам?" (Do you prefer the beach or the mountains?)
- B) "Твої очі нагадують мені красу зоряної ночі." (Your eyes remind me of the beauty of a starry night.)
- C) "Ти знаєш, що за цим місцем стоїть чудова історія?" (Did you know this place has the best story behind it?)
- D) "Хотів/хотіла б випити щось зі мною?" (Would you like to grab a drink with me?)

3. When giving a compliment, you're most likely to say:

- A) "Цей колір тобі дуже пасує!" (That color looks great on you!)
- B) "Ти найцікавіша людина, яку я зустрічав/зустрічала." (You're the most fascinating person I've met.)
- C) "У тебе дуже особлива енергія." (You have a very special energy.)
- D) "Ти мені подобаєшся, і я хочу, щоб ти знав/знала це." (I like you, and I want you to know.)

4. When faced with a moment of silence, you usually:

- A) Crack a light joke to break the tension.
- B) Share an anecdote that brings out your sentimental side.
- C) Smile and wait for the right moment to make a subtle comment.
- D) Ask a direct question to keep the conversation going.

Results and Insights

- **Mostly A's – Playful Flirt**

    You enjoy using humor and lighthearted conversation to create a fun and relaxed atmosphere. In Ukrainian culture, a playful approach is welcomed, especially in social settings like bars and parties. Use this to your advantage but be mindful of when to switch to a more serious tone.

    Tips for Playful Flirts: Lean into your natural wit and humor, but balance it with genuine interest when conversations deepen. Practice phrases like, *"Ти завжди знаєш, як мене розсмішити"* (You always know how to make me laugh).

- **Mostly B's – Romantic Flirt**

    You're drawn to classic and heartfelt expressions of admiration. In most places, a romantic style can be charming and effective, as it shows sincerity and passion.

    Tips for Romantic Flirts: Embrace your poetic nature but stay attuned to cues that indicate whether the other person is comfortable with this level of intensity. Try phrases such as, *"Ти як ожила поема"* (You're like a poem brought to life).

- **Mostly C's – Subtle Flirt**

  You prefer a more nuanced approach, using body language and subtle cues to communicate your interest. This style can be appreciated in more conservative regions, where directness might be seen as too forward.

  Tips for Subtle Flirts: Don't be afraid to step out of your comfort zone and express your interest more clearly when the moment calls for it. Simple phrases like, *"Мені подобається бути поруч із тобою"* (I like being near you) can bridge subtlety and clarity.

- **Mostly D's – Direct Flirt**

  You're confident and straightforward, making your intentions clear from the start. In most places, being direct yet respectful is seen as attractive and confident.

  Tips for Direct Flirts: Maintain your boldness but soften it with warmth and openness to avoid coming across as too intense. Use expressions like, *"Я хочу краще тебе пізнати, це нормально?"* (I want to get to know you better, is that okay?).

How to Use Your Flirting Style

Understanding your natural style can help you leverage your strengths and adapt to different social settings. Here's how to enhance or balance your approach:

- **If You're Playful:** Add a touch of sincerity when the conversation becomes more meaningful.

- **If You're Romantic:** Dial down the intensity if you sense it might be overwhelming for the other person.

- **If You're Subtle:** Practice expressing your feelings more openly to avoid confusion.

- **If You're Direct:** Incorporate moments of lightness or humor to soften your approach.

Exercise:

Now that you know your flirting style, practice a conversation or role-play with a friend or in front of a mirror. Try using one or two tips to balance your approach and adapt it to different scenarios.

Understanding and enhancing your flirting style will help you feel more confident, authentic, and adaptable in any Ukrainian-speaking environment.

BUILD YOUR OWN FLIRTY CONVERSATION

Building a conversation that flows naturally and captures the interest of the other person is an essential skill in flirting. This section will guide you through crafting your own flirty dialogue using common Ukrainian phrases and questions. You'll find examples, tips for making interactions engaging, and an exercise to help you put your new skills into practice.

Phrases and Questions to Use in Your Conversations

Below is a curated list of phrases and questions that can help you start, maintain, and enrich a conversation:

Starting the Conversation:

- **Привіт, як справи сьогодні?**
  (Hi, how are you today?)

- **Ти часто сюди приходиш?**
  (Do you come here often?)

- **Радій/рада бачити тебе тут.**
  (I'm glad to see you here.)

Showing Interest and Engaging:

- Мені подобається, як ти говориш про [їхню тему інтересу].
  (I love how you talk about [their topic of interest].)

- Що завжди змушує тебе усміхатися?
  (What's something that always makes you smile?)

- У тебе чудове почуття гумору.
  (You have an amazing sense of humor.)

Transitioning to Personal Topics:

- Розкажи мені більше про свої захоплення.
  (Tell me more about your hobbies.)

- Яке твоє улюблене місце для відпочинку?
  (What's your favorite place to relax?)

- Якби у тебе був ідеальний день, яким би він був?
  (If you had a perfect day, what would it be like?)

Responding to Keep the Conversation Flowing:

- Це звучить чудово! Мені теж подобається [схожа діяльність або тема].
  (That sounds great! I also love [similar activity or topic].)

- Як цікаво, я ніколи не думав/думала про це таким чином.
  (How interesting, I'd never thought of it that way.)

- Я б хотів/хотіла дізнатися про це більше.
  (I'd like to hear more about that.)

Ending the Conversation Gracefully:

- Було приємно з тобою поспілкуватися, сподіваюся, ми зможемо це повторити.
  (It was a pleasure talking to you, I hope we can do it again.)

- Дякую за таку приємну розмову.
  (Thank you for such a pleasant conversation.)

- До зустрічі, підходить?
  (See you soon, sound good?)

Example Conversation

Here's a sample dialogue to illustrate how you can piece these phrases and questions together for a natural, engaging conversation:

Setting: You meet someone at a social gathering.

You: Привіт, як справи сьогодні?
(Hi, how are you today?)

Them: Дуже добре, дякую. А у тебе?
(Very well, thank you. And you?)

You: Добре, дякую. Радій/рада бачити тебе тут. Ти часто відвідуєш такі заходи?
(Good, thank you. I'm glad to see you here. Do you come to these events often?)

Them: Ні, я тут вперше, але я люблю живу музику.
(No, it's my first time, but I love live music.)

You: Який збіг! Мені це теж подобається. У тебе є улюблений гурт?
(What a coincidence! I love it too. Do you have a favorite band?)

Them: Так, мені подобається [назва гурту].
(Yes, I like [band name].)

You: Це чудовий вибір. У тебе чудовий музичний смак.
(That's a great choice. You have amazing music taste.)

Them: Дякую. А ти? Яку музику ти любиш?
(Thank you. And you? What kind of music do you like?)

You: Трохи всього, але я люблю джаз. Я б із задоволенням поговорив/поговорила про це наступного разу. Хотів/хотіла б випити щось разом і продовжити розмову?
(A bit of everything, but I love jazz. I'd love to talk more about this next time. Would you like to grab a drink one day and continue the conversation?)

Tips for Making the Interaction Engaging

1. **Active Listening:** Pay attention to what the other person says and respond with genuine interest.

2. **Balance Questions and Comments:** Avoid making the conversation feel like an interview by mixing questions with personal insights or reactions.

3. **Adapt to the Flow:** Be flexible and ready to shift topics naturally based on their responses.

Exercise: Create Your Own Flirty Conversation

Using the phrases and tips provided, craft a conversation that you might have in a casual or romantic setting. Consider these guidelines:

- Start with a friendly greeting.
- Use at least two engaging questions or compliments.
- Transition smoothly between topics.
- End with a closing that leaves the conversation open for future interactions.

Evaluation: After writing your conversation, read it aloud or practice with a partner. Reflect on the flow and whether it feels natural and engaging. Adjust phrases as needed to make your dialogue sound more authentic and comfortable for you.

FIRST DATE ICEBREAKER GAME

First dates can sometimes feel a little daunting, especially when you're trying to make a great first impression. Having some fun and lighthearted icebreaker questions in your arsenal can help set the tone and create a relaxed atmosphere. In this section, you'll find a selection of 'Would you rather' questions, rapid-fire prompts, and conversation starters in Ukrainian that you can use to break the ice and keep the conversation flowing smoothly.

Fun 'Would You Rather' Questions in Ukrainian

These questions are perfect for sparking laughter and revealing interesting insights about each other:

- **Ти б хотів/хотіла подорожувати в минуле чи майбутнє?**
  (Would you rather travel to the past or the future?)

- **Ти б волів/воліла мати здатність літати чи бути невидимим/невидимою?**
  (Would you rather have the ability to fly or be invisible?)

- **Ти б обрав/обрала вечерю з улюбленою знаменитістю чи довічні квитки на улюблені концерти?**
  (Would you rather have dinner with your favorite celebrity or have lifetime tickets to your favorite concerts?)

- **Ти б хотів/хотіла жити на пляжі чи в горах?**
  (Would you rather live at the beach or in the mountains?)

- Ти б волів/воліла більше ніколи не їсти десерт чи більше ніколи не дивитися улюблений фільм?
  (Would you rather never eat dessert again or never watch your favorite movie again?)

Tip: Use these questions with a playful tone and be ready to share your own answers. This encourages your date to open up and keeps the conversation lively.

Rapid-Fire Prompts in Ukrainian

Rapid-fire questions are a great way to keep the energy up and discover fun facts about each other quickly. Here are a few to try out:

- Кава чи чай?
  (Coffee or tea?)

- Дощовий день чи сонячний день?
  (Rainy day or sunny day?)

- Бойовики чи комедії?
  (Action movies or comedy?)

- Поїздка в місто чи втеча на природу?
  (City trip or nature getaway?)

- **Танці на вечірці чи слухання розслаблюючої музики вдома?**
  (Dancing at a party or listening to relaxing music at home?)

Tip: These questions are best used during a pause in conversation or when you want to keep things light and dynamic. Answering quickly without overthinking helps maintain a fun atmosphere.

Conversation Starters in Ukrainian

Use these starters to dig a bit deeper and learn more about your date's personality, interests, and stories:

- **Який твій улюблений спогад з дитинства?**
  (What's your favorite childhood memory?)

- **Якби ти міг/могла мати будь-який талант, який би ти обрав/обрала?**
  (If you could have any talent, which would you choose?)

- **Яке твоє місце мрії для подорожі і чому?**
  (What is your dream travel destination and why?)

- **Яка найкраща порада, яку ти коли-небудь отримував/отримувала?**
  (What is the best advice you've ever received?)

- **Якби ти міг/могла їсти лише одну страву до кінця життя, що б це було?**
  (If you had to eat only one dish for the rest of your life, what would it be?)

Tip: These questions are designed to move beyond surface-level small talk and help you create a meaningful conversation that allows you both to share more about yourselves.

Creating a Relaxed, Fun Atmosphere

To make your date feel comfortable:

- **Be genuine:** Use a warm tone and maintain eye contact when asking these questions.

- **Share your own stories:** Be open and willing to answer your own questions. This shows vulnerability and encourages your date to share as well.

- **Listen actively:** Respond with interest, using phrases like *"Це цікаво!"* (That's interesting!) or *"Я цього не знав/знала, розкажи мені більше"* (I didn't know that, tell me more).

Practice Exercise

Find a partner or friend and practice using these questions in a mock date setting. Take turns asking and answering questions, observing how the conversation naturally flows. Reflect on the following:

- Did your answers spark further discussion?
- Which questions were most engaging, and why?
- How did the questions set the mood for the conversation?

Practicing these games can make you feel more comfortable and confident during a real date, ensuring that your interactions are smooth, engaging, and memorable.

CHAPTER NINE:
PUTTING IT ALL TOGETHER

Congratulations on reaching the final chapter of *How to Flirt in Ukrainian!* By now, you've explored and practiced the art of flirting, from initial encounters and lighthearted banter to expressing affection and navigating delicate moments. You've equipped yourself with a wealth of vocabulary, cultural insights, and strategies to approach interactions with confidence and sincerity. This chapter will tie it all together, reinforcing the key takeaways from the book and providing encouragement for your next steps as you put your new skills into action.

Reflecting on Your Journey

Learning how to flirt in a new language is no small feat—it's a combination of mastering the language itself, understanding cultural nuances, and building your personal confidence. By investing time into this book, you've committed to enriching your communication skills in a way that goes beyond the textbook phrases and formal conversations. Flirting is, at its core, about connection, and you now have the tools to make meaningful connections with others while embracing the unique charm of the Ukrainian language.

Take a moment to reflect on your journey:

- **Vocabulary Mastery:** You've gained a repertoire of essential words and phrases, from compliments and conversation starters to polite rejections and expressions of affection. Practice these words regularly so that they feel natural when the time comes to use them.

- **Cultural Understanding:** Flirting isn't a universal approach. In Ukrainian culture, subtlety and sincerity often play a significant role. Whether it's the warmth of a friendly conversation, a compliment delivered with genuine intent, or the respectful charm valued in more formal settings, adapting your style to fit Ukrainian cultural norms is essential for creating meaningful connections.

- **Confidence-Building Techniques:** From handling shyness to responding gracefully to rejection, you now have strategies to stay composed and positive. Confidence isn't just about knowing what to say; it's about how you present yourself and respond in any situation.

The Art of Natural Flirting

One of the main lessons of this book has been understanding that effective flirting is more than memorizing phrases—it's about making those phrases your own. Personalization and authenticity are what set apart a charming exchange from a forgettable one. Remember:

- **Listen Actively:** True connection stems from listening more than talking. Responding thoughtfully to what the other person says shows that you value their perspective and encourages deeper conversations.

- **Adapt Your Approach:** While some settings call for subtle, polite language, others may welcome humor and a playful tone. Flexibility is key to navigating different social settings and adjusting your approach as you get to know the other person.

- **Stay True to Yourself:** The best flirts are genuine. Use phrases and expressions that feel natural to you, and don't be afraid to inject your personality into your conversations.

Putting Your Skills into Practice

Flirting in Ukrainian may feel daunting at first, but remember that practice is your greatest ally. Here are some final tips to keep in mind as you integrate what you've learned:

1. **Start Small:** Practice with friends or language partners to build your comfort level. Begin with casual compliments or conversation starters and work your way up to deeper interactions.

2. **Observe and Learn:** Watch movies, TV shows, or social media content from Ukrainian culture. This will help you pick up on nuances, popular phrases, and current trends in how people interact.

3. **Keep Practicing:** Regularly revisit the exercises and scenarios in this book. Repetition will reinforce what you've learned and help you approach real-life situations with greater ease.

4. **Reflect on Your Experiences:** After each interaction, think about what went well and what could be improved. Celebrate your progress, no matter how small, and continue refining your approach.

Embracing the Journey Ahead

Flirting in Ukrainian is as much about the journey as it is about the end result. It's about enjoying the process of communicating in a new way, embracing cultural differences, and discovering more about yourself in the process. With each conversation, you'll gain more than just language skills—you'll grow your confidence, adaptability, and interpersonal abilities.

Don't be discouraged if not every interaction goes perfectly. Remember, even native speakers don't get it right every time. The most important thing is that you're putting yourself out there, learning, and having fun along the way.

A Final Word of Encouragement

As you continue to hone your skills, remember that flirting is meant to be light, enjoyable, and a way to connect with others. You now have the knowledge and tools to make those connections in Ukrainian-speaking settings, whether you're meeting someone for the first time, texting, or engaging in deeper conversations.

Approach each interaction with curiosity, warmth, and an open heart. Trust in what you've learned, and don't be afraid to step out of your comfort zone. You have everything you need to navigate the world of Ukrainian flirting with confidence and authenticity.

With your newfound skills, go out and create memorable, engaging, and meaningful conversations. *Удачі та насолоджуйся цією подорожжю!* (Good luck and enjoy the journey!)

- *Adrian Gee*

Printed in Great Britain
by Amazon